CLICK2CHANGE

A BETTER WORLD AT YOUR FINGERTIPS

MICHAEL NORTON

TURNAROUND

Click2Change: A Better World at Your Fingertips
by Michael Norton

First published in Great Britain in 2012 by Turnaround Books in association with Centre for Innovation in Voluntary Action and The Big Issue Foundation

Turnaround Books, Unit 3 Olympia Trading Estate, Coburg Road, London, N22 6TZ
www.turnaround-uk.com

Centre for Innovation in Voluntary Action
9 Mansfield Place, London NW3 1HS, UK
Registered charity number 1122095
www.civa.org.uk and www.click2change.net

The Big Issue Foundation
1-5 Wandsworth Road, London SW8 2LN
Registered charity number 1049077
www.bigissue.org.uk

The right of Michael Norton too be identified as the author of this work has been asserted by him in accordance with the Copyright, Design and Patents Act 1988.

Design and illustration by Laugh It Off: www.laughitoff.co.za

Printed by the Russell Press, Nottingham

SOME INSPIRING QUOTATIONS FOR PEOPLE WHO ARE THINKING ABOUT CHANGING THE WORLD:

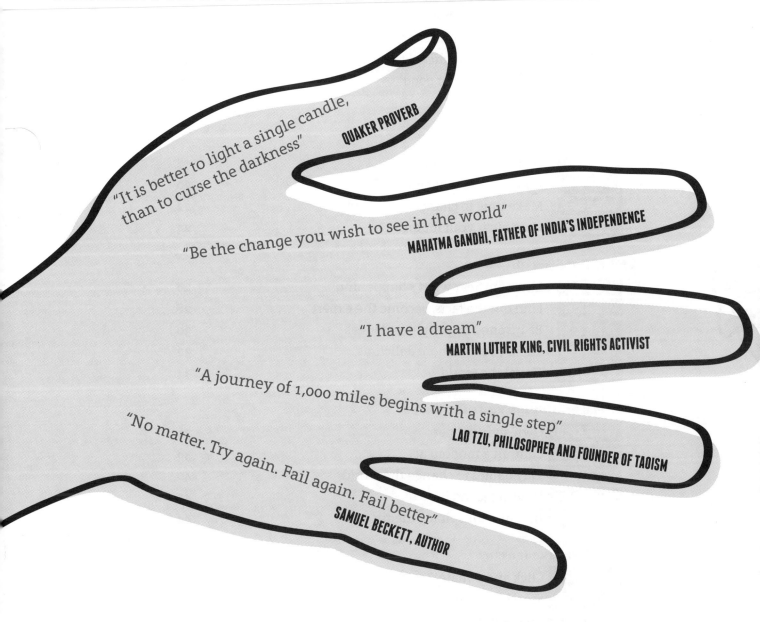

"It is better to light a single candle, than to curse the darkness"
QUAKER PROVERB

"Be the change you wish to see in the world"
MAHATMA GANDHI, FATHER OF INDIA'S INDEPENDENCE

"I have a dream"
MARTIN LUTHER KING, CIVIL RIGHTS ACTIVIST

"A journey of 1,000 miles begins with a single step"
LAO TZU, PHILOSOPHER AND FOUNDER OF TAOISM

"No matter. Try again. Fail again. Fail better"
SAMUEL BECKETT, AUTHOR

CIVA

Centre for Innovation in Voluntary Action is a UK-based charity founded in 1995 which promotes active and engaged communities and encourages and supports social entrepreneurs to create and lead change.

The Big Issue and its associated charity *The Big Issue Foundation* support homeless people by providing them with opportunities to earn and income and re-engage with mainstream society through selling its weekly street publication.

CONTENTS

WHAT'S IN THE BOOK

Welcome to "*Click2Change: A Better World at Your Fingertips*". This book provides you with 52 different topics for things that you can do that will help create a better world – just by accessing the internet. You don't even need to get off your backside to make a difference. So no excuses!

That's one topic and several ideas for what to do for each week of the year. Some of the topics are glaringly obvious; others a little more unusual or unexpected. The 52 topics are divided into these nine themes:

1. *Test yourself.* To start off, see whether you have what it takes to become a world-changer (you almost certainly do!). Discover how environmentally responsible you are. And make sure that you can find time to change the world.

2. *Find out more.* Be curious. Use your computer or *iPad* to find out the facts, access ideas and get inspiration for your world-changing efforts.

3. *Indulge your fantasies.* Next have a bit of fun. Do things such as change the world at random or own a virtual pet (which will help you lower your carbon emissions).

4. *Give it away.* Use your computer to invest or donate money to enable others to create change. You can also give away all your unwanted stuff, or even donate yourself and your body parts when you die.

5. *Become an online volunteer.* Instead of or as well as giving money, you can give time to change the world. Become an e-activist, a virtual volunteer, an online mentor.

6. *Get the message out.* Get t-shirts printed with slogans of your choice. Get your book published. Build your own website. Become a blogger… or even an online guru.

7. *Link up in cyberspace.* Join with others by sharing your books, your broadband and even your computer. Or interact with others through social networking and meet-ups.

8. *Campaign for change.* Organise a campaign from your bedroom. Mobilise millions. Take urgent action and give rapid responses in emergencies. Send petitions to political leaders to goad them into action.

9. *Be an ethical consumer.* There are all sorts of options for buying things without compromising your values. As an online shopper you can make choices for good in what you purchase and even with the credit card you use.

The book ends with a miscellany of topics. You can explore doomsday scenarios to see if there will be a world left to change; if you feel that it's not worth saving anyway, why not escape to Mars? But if you feel that our world really can deal with its problems and if you are prepared to contribute your time and energy towards this, then pledge to make a difference – you could even consider resigning your job to become a full time activist for change.

HOW TO GET STARTED

Almost everyone is prepared to do something that will make our world a bit better – however small and especially if it does not involve too much effort! The problem is that we may not know what to do or where to get started. If this is the case for you, then you're fortunate… *this book has been written specially to for you!*

You can go through the book systematically, week by week, starting at the beginning and ending 52 weeks later. You can sign up for a daily tweet or e-mail, and receive a suggested daily action. You can read the book from cover to cover, and explore the ideas that really inspire you. Or you can just select the topics that take your fancy.

However you decide to use the book, find things to do … and do them.

CAN YOU REALLY MAKE A DIFFERENCE?

Can one person really change the world just with a click? Well, yes they can, even if it's just a small difference. But if lots of people do lots of little things, this will add up to a huge difference.

Once you start doing little things and you begin see that what you are doing really is having an impact, then you might start to think about what more you can do… and go on to do bigger and better things. This might spur you on to developing your own ideas for changing the world – and then putting these ideas into practice. Who knows what this might lead to? You might even become a future Muhammad Yunus (who won the *Nobel Peace Prize* in 2006 for creating the *Grameen Bank*).

Read this book. Get lots of ideas from it. Go and do something. What and how much is entirely up to you. But make sure that you have fun whatever it is you decide to do.

Michael Norton
January 2012

HOW THE INTERNET IS CHANGING EVERYTHING

The internet is having a profound impact on our lives. Imagine a world without e-mail, without online shopping and reservations, without *Facebook* or *Twitter*, without being able to *Skype* anyone anywhere for free and see them as you talk. The internet is not only changing how we live, it is also changing how we speak. *"Googling"*, *"Social Networking"*, *"Apps"* and *"Wikis"* have entered our vocabulary. The internet is evolving all the time. New applications, new functions and new services come on stream daily.

John Reed, an American journalist, was in Russia at another interesting time. He saw the 1917 Communist revolution as it was happening, and wrote about it in his book *"Ten days that shook the world"*. We are seeing the IT revolution as it is happening and affecting every aspect of our lives.

TEN WAYS IN WHICH THE INTERNET IS SHAKING UP OUR WORLD

(1.) **The internet provides instant access** to information on almost everything. Just type a few letters into *Google* and you can search billions of internet pages to find the information you are looking for.

(2.) **The internet allows information to be shared.** On many websites and blogs, you can participate in the information flow by adding your own information or point of view. You can review books on *Amazon* or provide holiday information on *Trip Advisor* or just tell your *Facebook* friends the things you like.

(3.) **The internet enables people to join communities and networks.** You can join a *Critical Mass* to promote an environmentally sensible mode of transport. You can *Stitch 'n Bitch*, chatting about this and that whilst you knit. You can become part of a *Flashmob* happening in your city. You can *MeetUp* on almost anything.

(4.) **The internet enables democratic conversations.** Instead of information managed by editors with the information flowing from the top downwards, you can now express your opinions and be heard. You can become a citizen journalist, pioneered by *OhMyNews* in Korea. You can post items or add comments on websites such as *Digg.com* and *Metafilter.com*.

(5.) **The internet facilitates collaboration.** Read the book *"Wikinomics"* which shows how pharmaceuticals are being designed, motorcycles built and gold fields discovered by people working together. *Wikipedia* and *Linux* are two prime examples of this "crowdsourcing" approach.

(6.) **The internet empowers grass roots activism.** Whether it's *Plane Stupid* fighting a third Heathrow runway or Barack Obama's *"Yes We Can"* campaign for the US Presidency or *Greenpeace* campaigning against the tar sands ecological disaster in Canada, or *Avaaz* campaigning on topical issues, people can act together in common purpose.

(7.) **The internet is shrinking the world.** Ideas can spread in an instant. A good example is *Free Hugs*. Juan Mann arrived home in Australia with nobody to welcome him at the airport. He posted a video of his *Free Hugs* idea on *YouTube* in 2006. This was viewed over 10 million times in the following 3 months, and led to *Free Hugs* groups being set up all around the world.

(8.) **The internet collapses time.** A tsunami strikes Japan, people take to the streets in Cairo. Immediately information is *Tweeted* or posted on *YouTube*. People know what's happening, and can take immediate action.

(9.) **The internet creates greater choice.** A bookstore has limited shelf space for its stock; but an internet bookstore such as *Amazon* has no such limitations. This leads to *"The Long Tail"*, where small quantities of large numbers of items can be archived and sold.

10. *The internet encourages greater transparency.* Governments, leaders and corporations can be held to account much morez effectively, because information can be put in the pubic domain, for example through *WikiLeaks*, and people can send a flood of e-mails via a rapid response network whenever a major issue arises, such as through *Amnesty* in response to a human rights abuse.

HOW THE INTERNET CAN HELP US CHANGE THE WORLD

The internet has now become an indispensable tool for helping us change the world.

With just a click, you can find out about almost everything… you can connect with other people and other organisations … you can share experiences, knowledge and ideas… you can meet up with others… you can circulate photographs and videos… you can engage in issues and get involved in discussions… you can collaborate with others to work on problems together, and together you can do far more than any single individual can do… you can raise money, and you can also give money, sometimes at no cost to yourself… you can add your point of view to discussions in the mainstream media or in planning a campaign, so that what concerns you and people with similar views is taken account of… you can mobilise people around the issues you care about… you can bombard powerful people with calls to action to the point where they can no longer ignore you… you can even write to the President of the Free World.

To give you a flavour of what's in this book, here are just a few creative ways in which the power of the internet is being harnessed to change the world for the better:

✳ You can now support one person in a developing country with a small loan which will provide them with a hand up. They keep in touch with you and tell you their progress. And when their micro-business succeeds, they repay you. You can then have your money back, or you can lend it to somebody else to give another person a hand up. This direct person-to person link shows you that your support can make a real difference to someone's life. So instead of eating out tonight in a restaurant, why not spend the same amount money on changing someone's life? Do this at: **www.kiva.org**. Then decide which gives you more pleasure.

  Or if you don't want to support just one individual, you can adopt a whole village by becoming a virtual volunteer, when you can use your skills to help solve their problems. Sign up to become a "good neighbour" at **www.nabuur.com**

✳ You can join a rapid response network and add your voice to millions of others to create a powerful response to some global issue. It might be a human rights issue or the failure of our elected politicians to take the threat of global warming seriously. Sign up to an organisation such as *Amnesty International* or *Greenpeace* to become a rapid responder. Or sign up to organisations such as *Avaaz*, *38 Degrees* or *GetUp* which now mobilise millions on issues such as these in a matter of hours: **www.avaaz.org** or **http://38degrees.org.uk** or **www.getup.org.au**

✳ You can publish a book for as little as $10 where copies are only printed when people order them. This means that anyone anywhere can easily become a published author. Try it out at **www.lulu.com** or **www.blurb.com**. Or for just a few dollars, you can use the internet to design and produce a custom-made t-shirt or coffee mug with your very own world-changing message.

✳ You don't even need to bank with a bank. You can now lend your money direct to borrowers, and get a good return at relatively low risk. Ethical banks may become things of the past with the advent of "social lending". Try it out at **www.zopa.com** or **www.prosper.com**

✳ You can take a vocabulary test to improve your knowledge of the English language, and at the same time provide free rice to hungry people through the *World Food Programme*. Try this at

www.freerice.com. You may find it seriously addictive! If you can't manage the English or are not moved by the plight of the world's hungry, there are lots of other *"Click and Donate"* sites supporting a wide range of causes, such as **www.therainforestsite.com** where your click enables the purchase a square metre of rainforest.

✳ You can measure your carbon footprint on a carbon calculator. Then you can reduce it by deciding to look after a virtual pet instead of a real one, or by visiting somewhere in the world on *Google Earth* rather than actually going there.

✳ You can share your books with others by listing all your favourites on the *Library Thing*: **www.librarything.com**. Or you can leave a copy of your favourite book to be picked up by someone else for them to read and pass on, which is called *"Book Crossing"*: **www.bookcrossing.com**

The internet is inclusive. It is there for all of us to use and to benefit from. Whether you are young or old, whether you are able or have some sort of disability, whether you live in the rich world or the poor world, whether you are skinny or obese, whoever and however you are, and even if you are blind (where there are screen readers which enable you to listen to what appears on your screen), the internet enables you to participate as an equal.

But the internet requires more of you than simply being a passive browser, if you are to get the most out of it. You need to be actively participating in the processes of providing information, discussing issues and connecting with people. You need to create your own content and build your own networks around those issues that really concern you. The internet is a powerful agent for social change today. And it will be even more powerful tomorrow.

New Message ⊖ ▣ ⊗

File   Edit   View   Insert   Format   Tools   Message   Help

✉️
Send

From: click2change@gmail.com

To:

Cc:

Subject: URLs

www.kiva.org   www.zopa.com
www.nabuur.com   www.prosper.com
www.avaaz.org   www.freerice.com
http://38degrees.org.uk   www.therainforestsite.com
www.getup.org.au   www.librarything.com
www.lulu.com   www.bookcrossing.com
www.blurb.com   www.netaddiction.com

BEWARE OF BECOMING ADDICTED TO THE INTERNET!

Are you addicted to alcohol… tobacco… cocaine… heroin… gambling? Of course you're not.

But what about the internet, which this book is about? Compulsive internet use has now been identified as a mental health issue in some countries, including the US and also South Korea where over 90% of homes now have a broadband connection. Internet gaming, online gambling, frequenting chat rooms and fantasy worlds such as *Second Life*, social networking such as *Facebook* and incessant Tweeting are all giving people a PC bang which many then find hard to do without.

All this online activity is also isolating people within a world of virtual reality, where the most important thing to them is not human contact, but their computer screen, their *iPad*, their *iPhone*, their *iPod* and other electronic devices, all of which serve to create barriers to actual human contact whilst providing people with instant access to every nook and cranny of the world wide web, and which allows them to create a "personality" for themselves which might be quite different from who they really are.

The internet and the electronic world are there for good. But like all good things, you can have too much of it.

For example, as a planet we are spending 150 billion hours a year playing computer and video games. At the US minimum wage, that would be worth $1.5 trillion! The average young person will have spent 10,000 hours playing computer games by the age of 21 (that's equivalent to 8 years of formal schooling) – which is time that could otherwise be spent interacting in the real world.

Research in South Korea indicates that around 30% of young people under 18 are at risk of internet addiction. To address the problem, the South Korean government has built a national network of 140 counselling centres, set up treatment programmes in 100 hospitals and most recently paid for young people to go to a "boot camp" to try to get them to kick the habit. Each camp – called the *Jump Up Internet Rescue School* – lasts for 12 days and has around 16 participants; there is hard physical exercise plus group activities to encourage young people to form real relationships. It seems to be working.

Are you addicted to the internet or rapidly going that way?

Why not find out?

Take the Internet Addiction Test developed by the Centre for Internet Addiction Recovery.

This 20-item questionnaire measures mild, moderate, and severe levels of internet addiction. Here are the first five questions:

1. How often do you find that you stay online longer than you intended?
2. How often do you neglect household chores to spend more time online?
3. How often do you prefer the excitement of the internet to intimacy with your partner?
4. How often do you form new relationships with fellow online users?
5. How often do others in your life complain to you about the amount of time you spend online?

INTERNET ADDICTION: FOUR THINGS TO DO AND FIND OUT ABOUT

1. Look for signs of addiction – from mixed feelings of guilt and wellbeing whilst at the computer to thinking about when you will next be able to get online. You are most at risk if you are anxious or depressed, if you have an addictive personality (and other addictions such as drug use or gambling), if you lack social support or find it hard to leave the house, or if you are a teenager: **www.helpguide.org/mental/internet_cybersex_addiction.htm**

2. Take the *Internet Addiction Test* by going to *Self-Tests* at: **www.netaddiction.com**. Check out the website for ideas and resources that may help you kick the habit. There are also tests for cybersex/porn addiction, online gaming addiction, online auction addiction and for parents and partners of addicts. Take these tests too.

3. Do all these if you feel you are addicted:

   ✳ Keep a log of your time online day by day.

   ✳ Set goals for progressively reducing this.

   ✳ Replace your online activity with healthy activities, such as sport and exercise.

   ✳ If you're bored or lonely, try to think of ways of addressing this.

4. But don't give up the internet entirely. Remember that you *CAN* change the world with a click. So start reading this book and start clicking to change the world.

SET UP YOUR COMPUTER FOR GOOD

A good starting off point is to set up your computer in such a way that it will help you in your efforts to make a difference. Here are some simple things to do:

* **Share your broadband**. Using WiFi to access the internet, you can halve the cost of your broadband by sharing your connection with a neighbour. Or pay even less by sharing it with two or three neighbours. Or make it open, so that anyone nearby can access it without having to type in a password. A sharing world is a better world. And sharing your internet access could be a first step towards this *(see Chapter 38)*.

* **Sign up with a solar host**. The internet causes around 300 million tonnes of CO_2 to be released each year – this is as much as all the coal, oil and gas burned in Turkey or Poland, or more than half of the fossil fuels burned in the UK. The amount is growing, as more people use the internet and use it to do more things. You will be greener if you use a solar host, an internet service provider which uses solar energy as its source of power. There are several solar internet service providers – for example **www.solarhost.co.uk** – or just *Google* "solar hosting".

* **Get a URL that does some good**. For example, a dot.tv URL benefits the tiny Pacific island state of Tuvalu, which is one of the countries most threatened by global warming. Using dot.tv rather than dot.com for your domain name and internet address is distinctive (and certainly less selfish sounding than dot.me!). Register your domain at **www.watch.tv**. Find out more at **http://en.wikipedia.org/wiki/.tv**

* **Download and use free software** *(see Chapter 25)*. Use *Linux* rather than a *Microsoft* operating system; *OpenOffice* for creating documents and *Mozilla Firefox* for exploring the internet. The *Software Freedom* movement is about cooperation. You can bring these values right to the heart of your computer by using free software. There are more than 4,000 items you could use in the directory produced by the *Free Software Foundation*. **www.fsf.org**

* **Download a ScreenSaver** to remind you about some of the world's big issues. For example, your screen could remind you about:

    Human Rights: **www.amnesty.ca/activism/download_screensaver**
    Environment: **www.greenpeace.org/international/fungames/screensavers**
    Children and their needs: **www.unicef.org/about/who/index_23926.html**
    Climate change and the Antarctic: **www.wwfindia.org/help/fun_zone/index.cfm**

    Or you could use a photograph of yourself out campaigning for change.

* Your home page is what appears when you open your internet browser or when you hit the "Home" button. **Select a Click To Donate** website for your Home Page such as **www.freerice.com** or **www.thehungersite.com**. When the page comes up, click on the button to donate money for free *(see Chapter 15)*.

* **Rotate your home page**. Use the internet home page rotating tool *What Page* so that a different page appears each time you go to your Home Page. You can choose a maximum of 75 pages. So select some of the different Click-to-Donate sites that appeal to you, which will then appear in rotation. Most of these sites only allow you to click and donate once a day. So using this internet tool will increase the amount you donate through clicking. **www.whatpage.org**

* **Use a search engine which donates a part of its income to charity**. You don't have to use *Google*, or *Ask* or *Yahoo!* to search the internet. There are alternatives such as **www.everyclick.**

com *(see Chapter 16) where* a part of the advertising revenue generated from your searches is donated to charity.

✱ **Or use a search engine which uses a little less electricity** because it has been designed with white writing on a black screen: **www.blackle.com**.

✱ **Switch your computer off when you are not using it**, as this will save energy and reduce your carbon emissions. You can now buy a plug which automatically switches everything else off when you shut down your computer (and back on again when you start it up): **www.oneclickpower.co.uk**.

✱ **Or keep your computer switched on all the time** instead of switching it off, and use its computing power to help solve some of the world's biggest problems. This is done through a process called a "distributed network". Link up your computer to one. Then whenever your computer is not working for you, it could be modelling climate change, finding an AIDS vaccine, hunting for extraterrestrial life or finding the next prime number… plus a whole lot of other different things. You will surely be able to find something that interests you *(see Chapter 35)*. Check out: **http://distributedcomputing.info/projects.html**

Click2Change URLs:

www.solarhost.co.uk

www.watch.tv

http://en.wikipedia.org/wiki/.tv

www.fsf.org

www.freerice.com

www.thehungersite.com

www.whatpage.org

www.everyclick.com

www.blackle.com

www.oneclickpower.co.uk

http://distributedcomputing.info/projects.html

GOOD MOUSEKEEPING

MOUSE NOUS

1. Get yourself a comfortable chair to sit on. You'll be spending quite a lot of time in front of your computer.

2. Don't sit for hours peering at your monitor. Get up and exercise from time to time. Get some fresh air. Take a walk. Perhaps a random walk *(see Chapter 13)*.

3. Don't get addicted to the internet. There is a wider world out there, with lots of people and things to enjoy. If there is any danger, take action before it's too late *(see Page 13)*.

4. Think about having an internet-free day from time to time – a day when you don't even open your e-mails. Instead, telephone your friends… arrange to meet them… chat about life, the universe and everything.

5. Be curious. Set aside time to explore the internet without any particular end in mind. Check out interesting websites; follow links; see where this gets you and what you can find out. Type key words or phrases that interest you into *Google* – such as *"the end of the world"* – and see what comes up. You never know where this could lead.

6. You can change the world from your PC. But what you find out and what you do on your PC might inspire you to go out into the real world and do something there. The internet is an important tool for change… but it's not the complete answer.

7. Be an active contributor to discussions, post comments on blogs, create your own content. An interactive web requires creators as well as browsers.

8. Build your social networks of *Facebook* friends and *Twitter* followers and keep your profile up to date. But limit your time doing this.

9. If you come across something really interesting or have a great idea, spread this through your networks and contacts. The idea could go around the world in a flash.

10. Become a blogger *(see Chapter 33)*.

MOUSEKEEPING

1. Get yourself a distinctive e-mail address. For example, *Cyberstarlet* or *Bigmike @ Hotmail* or *Yahoo* or *Googlemail*, which will be easily remembered.

2. Have a memorable URL for your website, such as *www.moneycan.com* for your fundraising or *www.brand.me* for your leadership training work. Think about using a country indicator from Italy. Italy is dot.it – so you can change.it, fight.it, bulldoze.it. But you will need an Italian resident to set this up for you. Tuvalu is dot.tv – which seems quite cool *(see Page 14)*.

3. Set up your computer to do good in the world *(see Page 14)*.

4. Bookmark all your favourite websites, so you can return to them again and again. Use *Delicious* to do this *(see Chapter 8)*.

5. Use a spam filter to filter out all the rubbish, as opening it and reading it is just a waste of time. You're just not interested in bored girls, erectile dysfunction or fake Rolex watches. You know that

prizes from lotteries you haven't entered, invitations to appear in directories of famous people and requests to launder money are scams.

6. If you are receiving newsletters that you are not interested in, unsubscribe. This is usually quite simple to do.

7. Do what you can to protect your computer from viruses and worms. Don't open files from unknown senders. Install anti-virus software, and keep it up-to-date. This is less important for Mac users, as most attacks are on Microsoft operating systems.

8. Save what you write as you go along, just in case the programme crashes and the text can't be recovered.

9. File everything once you have dealt with it, rather than leaving it in your in-box. Have a special folder for interesting snippets.

10. Back up all your files and documents, so that the information is not lost if your computer crashes or is stolen.

11. Never give away your personal details, except when you know who you are interacting with. Someone could be stealing your identity… and your cash.

12. Have a credit card and open a *PayPal* account for making internet payments.

13. Remember your usernames and passwords. Try to keep them simple and the same for all your accounts. This may not always be possible, as often there are specific conditions (perhaps at least one letter and one figure, or no more than 12 characters), or your regular username may already be in use.

14. Gen up on the techniques of the internet. Ask other people how they do things, if you don't know. Go on courses, if it is important to you and you are dedicated enough.

52 WEEKS TO CHANGE THE WORLD

1. DEFINE YOUR IDENTITY

The starting point for setting out to change the world is you yourself. What are the issues that particularly concern you? What are your hopes for a better world? What are your motivations for wanting to do something? What attitudes and values do you bring? What do you want to achieve?

DISCOVER WHO YOU REALLY ARE

Hidden inside you, you may have strongly held prejudices that you might not even be aware of. You might be racist, sexist, ageist, homophobic or anti fat people. You might see people as stereotypes, rather than look under the surface and see them as individuals. You might jump to conclusions about them without any actual evidence

Tolerance of other people, of who they are and what they believe in, is an important ingredient of the better world that you hope to help create. So use one of the *Project Implicit Tests* developed at *Harvard University* to assess how tolerant you really are in relation to 90 different issues.

This test uses two concepts each having two opposites – for example, *age* (young or old) paired with *goodness* (good or bad). These are then paired in different configurations (for example *"Young and Good"* and *"Old and Bad"*. Words and images flash up on the screen, and you have to sort these into correct pairs. The more closely associated the concepts are in your own mind, the quicker you will respond. Your speed of response indicates your degree of hidden bias. You may be surprised what you find out about yourself! Take the test at: **https://implicit.harvard.edu/implicit**

FOUR SIMPLE WAYS OF OVERCOMING PREJUDICE

1. *Seeing is believing.* Experience the diversity of different cultures. For example, attend services at churches, synagogues, mosques and temples to learn about different faiths and denominations; understand their similarities and differences with your own beliefs.

2. *Mix it up.* Make a point of meeting and talking to people who are different from you.

3. *Understanding is everything.* Try to experience life from the perspective of others. Go out in a "wheelchair for a day" or eat in the dark at a "blind restaurant" to experience the daily aggravations of physical disability.

4. *Speak up* whenever you hear prejudice or people referred to as stereotypes. Say that such attitudes are just not acceptable.

TELL YOURSELF WHAT YOU WANT TO ACHIEVE

Sit down and write a letter to yourself setting out your concerns about the state of the world, your hopes and plans for changing it, and what actual pledges or promises you will make for doing things to make the world better.

Use *FutureMe* to email this letter to yourself. You decide when it will be sent. You could send it several times – perhaps after one year, and then again after three years and a third time, say, in ten years. When you receive these letters, you will probably have forgotten about your promises. Your letter will remind you, and could spur you on to do more and greater things. Do these:

✱ Browse some of the sample letters on the *FutureMe* website. Or

✱ *Buy their book "Dear Future Me".* And

✱ Sit down and write a letter to yourself at: **http://futureme.org**

CREATE A PROFILE

There are now literally hundreds of social networking sites, such as *MySpace* and *Orkut*. But the dominant sites are *Facebook* where you can connect with your friends, find new friends or join groups that interest you, new entrant *Google+* which launched in 2011, *Twitter* where you can send tweets of up to 140 characters to your friends, and *LinkedIn* where you can connect with professional contacts. Find out about the different sites and their popularity at: **http://en.wikipedia.org/wiki/List_of_social_networking_websites**

Choose the social network that best suits you. Sign up (If you haven't already done so). Create a profile for yourself (or update your existing profile). Make sure it reflects your concerns and your passion for creating a better world.

PROTECT YOUR IDENTITY

Your identity belongs to you, and only to you. It is important that you protect it. Identity theft is one of the world's fastest growing crimes. It's easily done by taking documents from your rubbish bin, or by contacting you by phone or e-mail telling you that you have won a prize or pretending to be your bank or credit card company. Only give out personal information if you are completely sure about the person making the request. This website has tips on keeping your identity safe: **www.identitytheft.org.uk**

And here's another thing you can do. Use an inkless thumbprint pad, and tell credit companies only to accept instructions from you if your signature is accompanied by a thumbprint. Find out more at **www.freeidprotection.co.uk** and order an inkless pad at **www.inklessprints.com**.

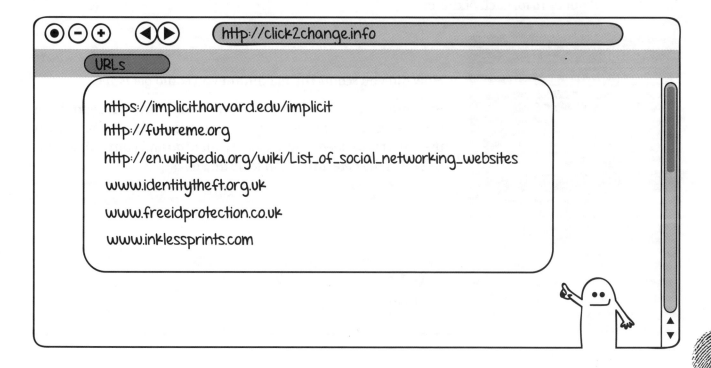

http://click2change.info

URLs

https://implicit.harvard.edu/implicit
http://futureme.org
http://en.wikipedia.org/wiki/List_of_social_networking_websites
www.identitytheft.org.uk
www.freeidprotection.co.uk
www.inklessprints.com

2. DO YOU HAVE WHAT IT TAKES?

Before starting out on your journey to change the world – even if you are doing this just from your desktop – it's worth thinking about the qualities and attributes you will need to succeed. You may already have them; or you may develop them as you go along. The first step is to realise that *you can do it*, and then to give yourself *a wake-up call to get going*.

Do you have these qualities and attributes?

* ✱ **Vision** to imagine a better world.

* ✱ **Creativity** to come up with a simple solution.

* ✱ **Passion** for what you plan to do.

* ✱ **Leadership skills** to mobilise people alongside you.

* ✱ **Ambition and drive** plus the will to succeed.

* ✱ **Determination and persistence** to overcome obstacles along the way.

* ✱ **Common sense** – become the expert by solving problems as you go along.

* ✱ **Self-belief**, knowing you can do it!

* ✱ **Get up and go**, taking risks and responding to challenges.

* ✱ **Good organising skills**, which you need to turn your ideas into action.

Getting started may well be the hardest thing to do. But remember the Lao Tzu quote: "*A journey of 1,000 miles begins with a single step*". Take that first step; then everything will follow. You're on your way!

RATE YOUR ABILITY TO CHANGE THE WORLD

Mark yourself out of 10 for each of these:

VISION	
CREATIVITY	
PASSION	
LEADERSHIP	
AMBITION	
PERSISTENCE	
COMMON SENSE	
SELF-BELIEF	
GET UP AND GO	
ORGANISING SKILLS	
TOTAL:	

How did you score? The maximum you could get is 100.

But your score doesn't matter much. Make mistakes. Learn from experience. Gain confidence from your successes. All you need at the outset is *an idea of what you want to do* and *your reasons for this*, plus the *determination to go and do it*.

GET A WAKE UP CALL FOR THE WORLD

Tip the Planet. This website provides tips for benefiting the planet. Browse the website. Add or edit tips. You will find the blindingly obvious (don't overfill the kettle), useful practical information (what fish not to buy) and the unusual (clean your leather shoes with banana skin, and some alternative uses for beer). **www.tiptheplanet.com**

Do the Green Thing. Sign up to this wacky website which encourages you to do some really simple things that benefit the environment – such as take a walk or go to bed early tonight. There are fun video clips and music to download, and lots of information and ideas for doing more. **www.dothegreenthing.com**

Explore 365 Ways to Change the World. This book provides an issue a day with facts and figures, inspiring stories and simple practical things you can do to make a difference. **www.365act.com**

Sign up to We Are What We Do for small actions that make a big difference: **www.wearewhatwedo.com**

Be inspired by Barack Obama's mantra "Yes We Can". Google this phrase; see what comes up.

OR JOIN THE SOCIETY OF PEOPLE WHO NEVER

If you decide that you are not going to change the world, then join *"The Society of People Who Never Got Around to Changing the World"*. This society does not yet exist. You will have to start it.

The idea of this is inspired by a Daily Telegraph rave review of a new production of *the "Sound of Music"*. A reader wrote saying that *"Now is the time to bring to the attention of music lovers the Society of People Who Have Not Seen The Sound of Music and Have No Intention of Doing So. I believe that I am the only member of this society"*. Other readers wrote in expressing a similar disdain for singing nuns, others proclaimed they had never seen *The Mousetrap* or had no intention of visiting *Ikea*, drinking *Coca Cola* or buying a lottery ticket.

Start a group on *Yahoo* or *MeetUp* or *Ning*. Design a membership certificate. Start to recruit people who like the world as it is, don't care about its problems and are too lazy anyway to do anything about them! And what about *Oldies Trashing the Planet* – because they want to enjoy themselves now and won't live to see the consequences.

Click2Change URLs

www.365act.com

www.tiptheplanet.com

www.dothegreenthing.com

www.wearewhatwedo.com

3. MAKE TIME TO CHANGE THE WORLD

Are you spending too much time in front of your computer dealing with e-mails, social networking, twittering, surfing the internet and playing games? Could you be using that time to help make a better world? Measure how are spending your time… and how much time you are wasting. Think of some ways creating more time in your life… which will give you even more time for changing the world.

In 19th Century Europe, working conditions were unregulated. The working day could range from 10 hours up to 16 hours six days a week. Religious sentiment ensured a day off for the Sabbath.

Robert Owen, a socialist pioneer, instituted a 10-hour day in his model industrial community of New Lanark in 1810. In 1817, he demanded an 8-hour day: *"Eight hours labour; Eight hours recreation; Eight hours rest."* Most employed people in the industrialised world had to wait until the 20th century for this. Today, the norm is a 35-hour week.

During the *Great Leap Forward* in China (from 1958 to 1961), Mao Zedong demanded that the people work at fever pitch. They had to run carrying heavy loads, whether it was freezing cold or blazing hot. They had to carry water up winding paths to irrigate the terraced fields. They had to keep the backyard steel furnaces going night and day. They literally had to move mountains.

Mao believed that work was good, and he hoped it would transform China. Mao set this *8-4-2-10 Regime* for Chinese workers and peasants:

> 8 hours sleeping
> 4 hours eating and breaks
> 2 hours studying… reading and discussing good Communist thought
> 10 hours working

Mao called this way of working *"Communist Spirit"*.

HOW DO YOU SPEND YOUR TIME?

There are 84,400 seconds in each day. Keep a diary of what you do for the next week. How much time did you spend on:

Working
Eating and breaks
Travel to work
Study, reading and hobbies
Sport and fitness
Shopping
Housework, cooking and child minding
Going out: to friends, to the cinema, to the pub, to a football match…
Leisure activities on your computer
Idling, including sitting in front of the TV, doing the crossword or SuDoku
Doing things for others and the community

Here are three simple ways of creating more time in your life.

HAVE AN INTERNET-FREE DAY

Turn your computer off for one day a year or one day a month, or even one day a week. There are *Dress Down Fridays*; so why not an *Internet-Free Day*? Leave your laptop at home, don't open your PC at the office. Instead, speak to real people in real time. Pick up the phone, rather than send an e-mail. Arrange to meet your friends. Get out into the real world… and get a life! Buy this domain; it's for sale: **www.internet-free-day.org**

Type these two URLs into your browser, and go to the *End of the Internet*: **www.cybermeme.net/end.html** and **www.1112.net/lastpage.html.** Tell your friends you have been there, and that they should go soon.

TURN OFF YOUR TV

We are all spending too much time "glued to the box". In the USA, children watch 1,023 hours of TV and spend just 900 hours in school each year.

TV may bring the world into your sitting room, but it is passive entertainment. So turn it off.

(1.) Reduce your own viewing by 50%. *White Dot* is the international campaign against TV. Read their survival guide *"Get a Life"* for what to do after you have turned your TV off: **www.whitedot.org**

(2.) Reduce the number of TVs in your home to just one. See Ken's smashed TV at: **www.turnoffyourtv.com/poemsessays/kenrubin.html** This may inspire you to smash your own!

(3.) Participate in *TV-Turnoff Week*: **http://unplugyourkids.com/turnoff-week**. Or go the whole hog with Digital Detox Week: **www.adbusters.org/campaigns/digitaldetox**. Both take place at the end of April.

(4.) Get a *TV-B-Gone* remote device that hangs on your key chain which can "turn off virtually any television" at home or in a public place. Point and press. It's that easy! **www.tvbgone.com**

STOP DOING SU-DO-KU

The *Su-Do-Ku* craze has spread around the world. Stop doing it. Spend the time doing something more useful. Half-an-hour-a-day equals 183 hours a year – which is nearly 8 days. You could achieve a helluva lot more than just completed Su-Do-Ku's in those eight days.

But think about this before you actually decide to give up: *"Researchers rank Su-Do-Ku puzzles among the top ten non-traditional ways to boost brain power (along with high-protein diets, listening to classical music, and having a lot of rest)."*

Click2Change URLs

www.internet-free-day.org
www.cybermeme.net/end.html
www.1112.net/lastpage.html
www.turnoffyourtv.com/poemsessays/kenrubin.html
www.whitedot.org
http://unplugyourkids.com/turnoff-week
www.adbusters.org/campaigns/digitaldetox
www.tvbgone.com

4. HOW BIG IS YOUR FOOTPRINT?

See whether you are consuming more than your fair share of the earth's resources. See how much you are contributing to global warming. Use the internet to measure *your footprint* – that is the impact of your lifestyle on the planet. Then think about what you can do to reduce it. Once you have done this, you will be in a better position to encourage others to adopt more sustainable lifestyles.

You have three important footprints:

✱ Your *Ecological Footprint* (your consumption of the world's resources).

✱ Your *Water Footprint* (your water use and what you cause to be used in a world that is fast running out of water).

✱ Your *Carbon Footprint* (your greenhouse gas emissions).

MEASURING YOUR ECOLOGICAL FOOTPRINT

A person's or a country's Ecological Footprint is the area of productive land that is required to produce all the food, energy and materials they consume and to absorb the wastes that they cause to be produced. Your footprint is measured in hectares of land per person.

The *Global Footprint Network* has produced a table of per capita footprints for all of the world's nations:

Top 8 footprints

United Arab Emirates	10.7
Qatar	10.5
Denmark	8.3
Belgium	8.0
United States	8.0
Estonia	7.9
Canada	7.0
Australia	6.8

Bottom 8 footprints

TimorLeste	0.4
Bangladesh	0.6
Afghanistan	0.6
Malawi	0.7
Palestinian Territories	0.7
Congo (DRC)	0.8
Mozambique	0.8
Pakistan	0.8

Selected other: UK 4.9, Switzerland 5.0, Russia 4.4, Japan 4.7, Germany 5.1, South Africa 2.3, China 2.2, Nigeria 1.4, India 0.9, Indonesia 1.2

Rich countries, not surprisingly, are at the top of the list, and poor countries at the bottom. In 2007, the world average footprint was 2.7 hectares (6.7 acres) per person. The total footprint of all of the world's population was 18.0 billion hectares, which compares with a total capacity of the world to support its population of 11.9 billion hectares. This shortfall will continue to widen as the world's population increases and as standards of living rise, although this will be compensated in part by technological advances, such as the harnessing of wind power and hydroponics.

This "sustainability gap" must be closed. The human race cannot continue indefinitely to take more from nature than nature itself can provide.

Check out the facts and find out about *Earth Overshoot Day*, the date in the year when the world overshoots its productive capacity for that year: **www.footprintnetwork.org /earthovershootday**

Measure your Ecological Footprint. Find out how many planets would be needed to sustain the earth's population if everybody lived at the same standard as you. Take the *Ecological Footprint Quiz* at: **www.myfootprint.org**

Check out the One Planet Living initiative and see if you can use only your fair share of the Earth's resources: **www.oneplanetliving.org**

MEASURING YOUR WATER FOOTPRINT

Your Water Footprint is the water you use directly and also the water you use indirectly through the foodstuffs and other consumables you purchase. Some of this water comes from regions of the world which are drying up. The world is growing increasingly short of water, so knowing your water footprint and taking steps to reduce it are both important.

Measure your Water Footprint at: **www.waterfootprint.org**. Check out the *Product Gallery* to find out how much water is required to produce some common foodstuffs and beverages. You'll be surprised!

MEASURING YOUR CARBON FOOTPRINT

Your Carbon Footprint is the amount of CO_2 that you cause to be emitted through home energy use, travel and consumption of goods and services. Every tonne you are responsible for contributes towards global warming.

The average Carbon Footprint per person in the UK is 9.37 tonnes.

Use a *Carbon Calculator* to measure your carbon footprint – your own footprint and the footprint of your whole family. Then see what you can do to reduce it. There are lots of ways of making a substantial reduction to your emissions.

Measure your Carbon Footprint. This carbon calculator is relatively simple to use: **www.carbon-footprint.com**. Put a widget on your website: **www.zerofootprint.net/engage-employees/widgets**

Make a pledge to reduce your carbon emissions. Join the *10:10 Campaign*: **www.1010global.org**.
And kids can lick global warming at: **www.lickglobalwarming.com**

Offset your carbon emissions by paying for things which reduce carbon emissions. This offset might be a tree that is planted, an emissions certificate withdrawn from circulation, or a new wind turbine. Buy a tonne of carbon at **www.carbonretirement.com**. Even if you decide to *offset*, you should still do what you can to *reduce* as well.

Check out Global Cool **www.globalcool.org** and **Acme Climate Action www.acmeclimateaction.com** for fun things to do.

www.footprintnetwork.org/earthovershootday
www.myfootprint.org
www.oneplanetliving.org
www.waterfootprint.org
www.carbonfootprint.com
www.zerofootprint.net/engage-employees/widgets
www.1010global.org
www.lickglobalwarming.com
www.carbonretirement.com
www.globalcool.org
www.acmeclimateaction.com

5. LISTEN IN, HEAR WHAT'S HAPPENING

Find out about the problems of the world and hear about some of the solutions. This is both interesting and important. Keeping up to date has never been easier. There is an information revolution taking place right now, with new ways of finding out, new ways of telling people and new ways of sharing information and ideas.

LISTEN IN

BBC World broadcasts many really great programmes on international development, health, environment, human rights, gender and other global issues. You can now listen on your *iMac, iPad, iPhone, iPod, PC* or *Blackberry*.

In 2009, around the world there were estimated to be:

* 234 million websites

* 126 million bloggers blogging

* 247 billion emails being sent every day

* 400 million active *Facebook* users

* 75 million active Twitter users sending 85 million Tweets each day

Check out the World Internet Project's surveys for the latest trends: **www.digitalcenter.org**

Do this to find out what is happening in the world. Get inspired to go out and do something. Come up with your own ideas for what needs to be done.

Tune in and enjoy. Listen in on your computer: **www.bbc.co.uk/worldservice** and find out the news at **www.bbcworld.com**. Check out the US equivalent, *National Public Radio*: **www.npr.org**

Download an App to listen in on anything from a laptop to a MP3 player. Each news outlet (such as the *BBC* or *Sirius Internet Radio*) will have its own App, and there are services as *WunderRadio* which aggregate news streams and podcasts from many broadcasters: **www.wunderradio.com** Check the Apps store for *Apple* or *Android* to find the right app for accessing the news you want.

Browse the latest news in words and pictures at *10x10*. This website displays the top 100 stories in the world in words and pictures every hour based on what's happening: **www.tenbyten.org**

GET GENNED UP

The mainstream media miss out on a lot of what's happening in the world. What is reported is usually from a "developed world perspective". Here are some good sources of information from a more radical perspective:

OneWorld.net: news and views from over 1,600 organisations promoting human rights and fighting poverty worldwide: **www.oneworldgroup.org**.

Indymedia: an alternative media network offering grassroots coverage of important social and political issues. **www.indymedia.org**

OhMyNews: a ground-breaking citizen journalism project which started in Korea in 2000 and has now gone international. It receives 150 stories a day from its network of 62,000 citizen contributors. **http://international.ohmynews.com**

Third World Network: research and information on global issues from a Southern perspective. **www.twnside.org.sg**

New Internationalist: issues of world poverty and inequality: **www.newint.org**

Resurgence: environment, ecology, creative living, spiritual wellbeing and sustainability. **www.resurgence.org**

Utne Reader reprints the best articles from over 2,000 alternative media sources. Some of this magazine is available on the web, some you need to subscribe to: **www.utne.com**

Truthout: independent voices on undercovered issues: **www.truthout.org**

SpotUs: If it's not being reported, find a journalist and crowdfund the cost of getting the issue researched and written about: **www.spot.us**

READ THE BLOGS

With tens of millions of people blogging all over the world every day, how can you find the blogs which are saying something interesting?

Global Voices guides you through the blogosphere by aggregating and amplifying the voices of credible bloggers around the world using an international team of volunteer authors, regional editors and translators. Each weekday they provide links to five or ten of the most interesting blog posts, and longer features highlighting current preoccupations of bloggers in different regions and countries. **http://globalvoicesonline.org**

Technorati lists its top 100 blogs from *Huffington Post* down at: **http://technorati.com/blogs/top100**

BlogDay is on 31st August. Spread the word about your favourite blogs: **www.blogday.org**. Post recommendations on your five favourites and five new blogs on your own blog and on your *FaceBook* page and to your *Twitter* followers.

GET ORGANISED

There's so much information about… but so little time to find it and read it. Use RSS *(Really Simple Syndication)* to get breaking news and the latest features delivered electronically to you from your favourite sources and on just the topics you are interested in – rather than having to hunt for what you want to find out about.

Get started with RSS. Start by downloading a *News Reader* programme: **www.rssreaders.com**

Use Netvibes to create a dashboard so you can access information more easily: **www.netvibes.com**

Tweetminster mines the tweets of opinion formers, influencers and MPs. Listen in to what they are tweeting on the key issues of the day: **http://tweetminster.co.uk**

Click2Change URLs
www.newint.org
www.resurgence.org
www.utne.com
www.truthout.org
www.spot.us
http://globalvoicesonline.org
http://technorati.com/blogs/top100
www.blogday.org
www.rssreaders.com
www.netvibes.com
http://tweetminster.co.uk

Click2Change URLs
www.digitalcenter.org
www.bbc.co.uk/worldservice
www.bbcworld.com
www.npr.org
www.wunderradio.com
www.oneworldgroup.org
www.tenbyten.org
www.indymedia.org
http://international.ohmynews.com
www.twnside.org.sg

6. FIND OUT THE FACTS, BECOME THE EXPERT

Is there an issue which really interests and concerns you – locally or nationally or globally? Is good information readily available about it? Do you have a particular perspective or can you assemble better data than anyone else?

With a little bit of *Googling*, you can find almost everything "with a click". This includes the facts, reports, other published information and the organisations doing something about it. Quite soon you will find that you know more about the issue than anyone else. *You will have become the expert!*

Here are three examples people doing just this:

Have a whale of a time: *"Whales are the world's largest, most ancient, highly intelligent and most peaceful creatures who have no natural predators… except humans. They live twice a human lifetime, and they dominate the oceans peacefully whilst maintaining their environment in a sustainable way. They don't kill larger and other intelligent life forms. The whale is our icon for success in evolution."* Irene Schleining, an Austrian artist living in London has created the *Whale of a Time* website, which has all the information you will ever need to know about whales and other endangered species. **www.whaleofatime.org**

Stop eating slave chocolate: *"So… knowing that some chocolate is made with slave labor, I don't see how someone could knowingly buy that chocolate again."* Steven Millman wrote to every chocolate manufacturer to ask if slave labour was used at any stage of the production process. This led to the *Stop Chocolate Slavery* website edited by Kyle Scheihagen which has all the information you need to know and suggestions for taking action: **http://vision.ucsd.edu/~kbranson/stopchocolateslavery/main.html**

The Iraq Bodycount: John Sloboda and Hamit Dardagan started to compile statistics from published information on civilian deaths in Iraq since the 2003 invasion in order to show the true cost of the war in human lives, which Western governments fail to do. *Iraq Body Count*: **www.iraqbodycount.org**

And here are two questions which you could start to think about:

* How many child slaves are there in the world and what are they forced to do? A lot of people would be interested in definitive information on this subject.

* Who is the most corrupt political leader in the world? *Transparency International* publishes an annual corruption index **www.transparency.org**, but building on this, you could create a hall of infamy on political leadership.

GET THE INFORMATION OUT

After compiling the information, your next step is to disseminate it as widely as possible. You could:

* Create a website, and through "search engine optimisation" make sure that it comes up top when people are searching for information on the subject. Read *"50 Ways to Make Google Love Your Website"* to find out what you need to do.

* Write a definitive article for *Wikipedia* or add to an existing article: **http://en.wikipedia.org**

* Write and publish an authoritative report. This will make you an "instant expert". You can publish your report on **www.lulu.com**

* Get endorsements from prominent people.

* Get publicity. Send out a press release and contact relevant journalists.

* Organise a stunt to get media attention.

It is surprisingly easy to become *THE EXPERT* if you really want to! Next try to become *THE PUNDIT* where you are asked to air your views regularly in the media.

COMPILE A FACTOID

This term was invented by Norman Mailer in his biography of Marilyn Monroe. He described a *Factoid* as *"facts which have no existence before appearing in a magazine or newspaper"* – something invented to influence public opinion. The term is also used to mean a small piece of true but insignificant information. For example, *"if the entire history of the earth lasted for only two days, human history would be only the last two seconds"* is a factoid.

Take a subject that interests you and compile ten factoids on it.

If you're stuck for a topic, then here's a suggestion. Tell people about the end of the world. Google *"End of the World"* and *"Doomsday Scenarios"* as your starting point.

* The world may end on one of these dates: **www.bible.ca/pre-date-setters.htm**

* The world may end for one of these reasons: **www.endofworld.net** or **www.exitmundi.nl**

CREATE AN ONLINE LENS

A lens is a personal focus on a topic that interests you. This could be anything from the crowd-owned *Ebbsfleet United* football club or living with juvenile diabetes.

Squidoo is a website hosting hundreds of thousands of lenses.

* You can create your own lens for *free*. It only takes a few minutes.

* Your lens can generate a royalty for your *favourite charity*.

Create a lens about something useful. Just click a button on the *Squidoo* homepage and you're on your way. **www.squidoo.com**

Click2Change URLs

www.whaleofatime.org
http://vision.ucsd.edu/~kbranson/stopchocolateslavery/main.html
www.iraqbodycount.org
www.transparency.org
http://en.wikipedia.org
www.lulu.com
www.bible.ca/pre-date-setters.htm
www.endofworld.net
www.exitmundi.nl
www.squidoo.com

7. BE INSPIRED

Using your brain to change the world is as important as using your wallet (giving money) or using your time (volunteering). One good way of getting ideas for what to do is to be inspired by other people's ideas and achievements... and there are lots of websites that will help you do this. Check out these websites:

TED: IDEAS WORTH SPREADING

TED conferences bring together some of the world's most fascinating thinkers and doers to discuss issues, ideas and solutions. You don't even have to attend a *TED* conference. The *TED* website contains hundreds of *TED* talks you can watch and share. Be inspired by the very different ideas of these three speakers, and browse the website to discover more: **www.ted.com**

The next Einstein will be African... Neil Turok, a South African-born theoretical physicist strongly believes that the solutions to the problems of Africa must come from Africans and that there is a severe skills shortage especially in maths and sciences. To address this, he started a 9-month postgraduate course using volunteer tutors. He is now creating maths institutes across the continent. **www.ted.com/talks/view/id/232** and **www.aims.ac.za**

A young Malawian builds a generator to provide light for his studies... When he was just 14 years old and studying at secondary school, William Kamkwamba built a small electricity-generating windmill from bicycle and other spare parts using rough plans he had found in a library book. His creativity and enterprise will amaze you, and his story has become the subject of a best-selling book *"The Boy who Harnessed the Wind"*. **www.ted.com/talks/lang/eng/william_kamkwamba_on_ building_a_windmill.html** and **http://williamkamkwamba.typepad.com**

When China will overtake the USA and become top nation... Hans Rosling looks at the economic growth of Asia and predicts to the hour the moment when China will overtake the USA in per capita wealth. **www.ted.com/talks/lang/eng/hans_rosling_asia_s_rise_how_and_when.html**

AN IDEA A DAY TO START THE DAY

The *Idea-a-Day* website launched in August 2000 publishes a daily good idea. All you do is sign up with your name and e-mail address. The idea will arrive daily in your e-mail in-box. You can also submit your own ideas, which will be posted on the website if they are imaginative enough. **http://ideaaday.org** Here are two ideas from the *Idea-a-Day* website:

✱ Allow voters in political elections to have one vote which they could cast either for or against a particular candidate.

✱ Empower the police to cordon off areas of natural beauty or cultural significance rather than just accident or crime scenes – perhaps to highlight a perfect patch of clover in Hyde Park or a handkerchief dropped by the Queen.

And reflect on the meaning of life: *The School of Life* is a place to step back and think intelligently about life, work, relationships, happiness and the wider world. They organise *Sunday Sermons* given by people with something to say. Read their thoughts: **www.theschooloflife.com/Sermons**

BE INSPIRED BY WHAT OTHER PEOPLE HAVE DONE

If there's a problem, we should try to look for a solution… whether it's gangs on the streets, the high incidence of teen pregnancy, elder abuse, Islamophobia, political corruption, youth unemployment, or an increasingly stressed-out society with rising levels of mental illness. Many of problems are complex, and the solutions not at all obvious. What is needed are people with ideas who are prepared to experiment and create the solutions we all need.

The *Nobel Peace Prize* honours contributions to peace, justice, and action on global problems. Recent winners have included:

> 2010, **Lu Xiaobo**, Chinese human rights activist
> 2006, **Muhammad Yunis**, microcredit innovator
> 2004, **Wangari Maathai**, creator of the Green Belt Movement in Kenya

The *Right Livelihood Award is an* "alternative Nobel Peace Prize". In 2010 the winners were:

> **Nnimmo Bassey** (Nigeria) for revealing the full ecological and human horrors of oil production.
> **Bishop Erwin Kräutler** (Brazil) for promoting the human and environmental rights of indigenous peoples
> **Shrikrishna Upadhyay** (Nepal) for community action to address poverty
> **Physicians For Human Rights-Israel** (Israel) for promoting health rights for all

Be inspired by what these and other winners have done:

> Nobel Peace Prize: **www.nobel.se/peace/laureates**
> Right Livelihood Awards: **www.rightlivelihood.org**

Check out these websites for more inspiring people and ideas:

✳ The *Ashoka Fellowship,* a world-wide network of around 2,000 creative and inspirational people all intent on creating a better world: **www.ashoka.org**

✳ The *Ashden Awards,* for sustainable energy solutions in the UK and the developing world: **www.ashdenawards.org**

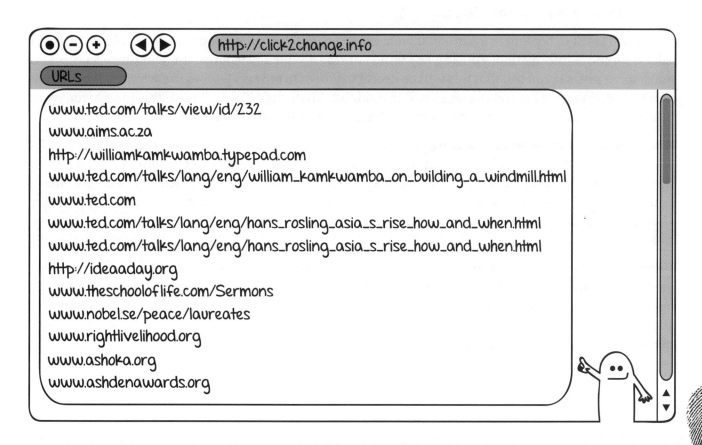

http://click2change.info

URLs

www.ted.com/talks/view/id/232
www.aims.ac.za
http://williamkamkwamba.typepad.com
www.ted.com/talks/lang/eng/william_kamkwamba_on_building_a_windmill.html
www.ted.com
www.ted.com/talks/lang/eng/hans_rosling_asia_s_rise_how_and_when.html
www.ted.com/talks/lang/eng/hans_rosling_asia_s_rise_how_and_when.html
http://ideaaday.org
www.theschooloflife.com/Sermons
www.nobel.se/peace/laureates
www.rightlivelihood.org
www.ashoka.org
www.ashdenawards.org

8. MAKE YOURSELF MORE DELICIOUS

Whenever you come across an interesting website, you will want to save the URL for future reference. Bookmarking is the way to do this. You can index it by giving it one or several tags. Tags are keywords which you use to categorise the website so you can sort and display your saved websites in an orderly way. This makes it is easier for you (and for others) to find what you are looking for.

You can create a "library" of all your favourite bookmarks using a social bookmarking service, and share your choices with other people. You can also alert them to an interesting website you have just come across by using *Twitter* or *Facebook*. If your friends take a look at it and like it, they might pass it on to their friends… and so it will spread. You can also use a social bookmarking website to explore other people's bookmarks and see how informative (and fun) their lists can be.

Some social bookmarking websites provide a RSS feed so that subscribers can be told about any bookmarks that have been recently added. As bookmarking has become more popular, extra features are being introduced – such as a facility for others to rate your bookmarks and make their own comments on them.

Find out more about bookmarking: **http://en.wikipedia.org/wiki/Social_bookmarking**

Watch a short video tutorial at: **www.commoncraft.com/bookmarking-plain-english**

HOW TO BECOME A SOCIAL BOOKMARKER

Delicious is the leading bookmarking service; it has now been taken over by *Yahoo*. Sign up at **www.delicious.com**. First create an account, then you will be asked to add a couple of buttons to your browser: *"Post to delicious"* which you will use for adding new websites, and *"My delicious"* which you will use for viewing your complete list.

When you want to bookmark a particular website, just click *"Post to delicious"* and a window will open asking for more information. You add key words or *"tags"* which categorise the website; you can also make some notes if you feel that this will be useful to you or to others viewing the website. The website will be added to your list and the tags listed in a sidebar. Then click *"Save"*. Repeat this process for every time you come across an interesting website. That's all there is to bookmarking.

An example of how bookmarking works: You have just found the **www.walkit.com** website which provides route maps for walking from A to B. When you save this, you might tag the site with these keywords: *"global warming" "alternative transport" "walking" "energy saving" "best websites"*. Your notes might say *"Fantastic website that promotes walking; maps available for all of London; shows calories burnt up and CO_2 emissions saved; you can ask for the most pleasant route or a circular route"*.

Play tag: Develop your tagging skills by playing *The ESP Game*. You are given an online partner. You are both shown a series of pictures. For each picture, each independently has to type in words could be tags for categorising that picture. The obvious tag words are already listed. Your task is to create additional tags. When you and your online partner come up with the same word, you score points and move on to tagging the next picture.

This game is fun to play, but it also generates new keywords which can be associated with particular images… and this enables images to categorised better and for search engines to find what people are looking for more easily. **www.gwap.com**

THREE THINGS YOU CAN DO

1. *Make yourself "Delicious":* Become an active bookmarker. Add to your list every time you come across something interesting. Set yourself a target of collecting 1,000 of the most interesting websites in the world, or 100 fantastic websites for global warming activists. Become a compulsive tagger, organising the websites into searchable categories. Provide access to your lists from your website. **http://delicious.com**

2. *Choose your all-time favourite website:* Then recommend this to everyone on your address book, to all your friends on *Facebook* and to your followers on *Twitter*. Tell them what you really like about it.

3. *Join the Open Directory Project:* This is the largest, most comprehensive human-edited directory of the internet, maintained by a global community of volunteer editors. You can submit sites and browse *Open Directory* to find what you need. Choose a topic that you know something about, and sign up as a volunteer editor. **www.dmoz.org**

Click2Change URLs:

http://en.wikipedia.org/wiki/Social_bookmarking

www.commoncraft.com/bookmarking-plain-english

www.delicious.com

www.walkit.com

www.gwap.com

http://delicious.com

www.dmoz.org

9. TRAVEL THE WORLD

You want to go travelling and see the world. But you're worried about your carbon emissions. Or you just can't spare the time to go away. Here's the perfect answer. Go wherever you want on your PC using aerial photographs on *Google Earth* **www.google.com/earth/index.html** and road maps on *Google Maps* **www.maps.google.com**

Start by visiting these two interesting but contrasting cities:

Mumbai, commercial capital of India, population 20.4 million (in 2011), financial and business capital of India, home of India's *Bollywood* film industry, attracts migrants from all over India who are seeking a better life.

Dharavi near Mumbai's airport is *"Asia's largest slum"*, estimated population 1 million in the midst of the wealth of Mumbai. The squalid living conditions might shock. Yet Dharavi is a hub of energy, industry, enterprise… and its residents all hope for a better tomorrow.

Los Angeles, population 4.1 million, home to some of the richest people on the planet, and with a large and growing Latino population. People are attracted by the warm climate, the glamour of *Hollywood* and the opportunity to live the "American Dream".

18th Street in East Los Angeles, not far from the palatial residences of Beverly Hills where film stars live in gated luxury, is the centre of LA's gangland culture – *"La vida loca"* or *"the crazy life"* with its daily gun crime, drugs scene and carjackings.

See the two sides of Mumbai Life in the best-selling *"Maximum City"* by Suketu Mehta **www.suketumehta.com** and the Oscar-winning film *"Slumdog Millionaire"*.
Catch up on Bollywood news: **www.planetbollywood.com**
Find out about LA gangland culture: **www.streetgangs.com/hispanic/18thstreet**. See the iconic *HOLLYWOOD* sign at: **www.hollywoodsign.org**
Catch up on Hollywood news: **www.hollywoodreporter.com**

DARK TOURISM

First tourism – travelling the world on vacation. Then green tourism – travelling more sustainably. Then social tourism – going somewhere to make a difference. Now dark tourism – visiting a world blackspot, such as…
Genocide: Auschwitz (Poland) or Kigali (Rwanda) or Darfur (Sudan).
Terrorism: the World Trade Centre (New York) or the airfield at Entebbe (Uganda) or the Munich Olympic Village.
Warfare: Iraq or Chechnya or the war graves in Northern France.
Nuclear fall out: Alamogordo (New Mexico) where the world's first atomic bomb was exploded, or Chernobyl (Ukraine), the site of the world's most serious nuclear accident, or Sellafield (UK) where nuclear waste is processed.
Famine: Zimbabwe or North Korea to see the *World Food Programme* in action.
Natural disasters: Miyagi (North-Eastern Japan) or Banda-Aceh (Indonesia) where tsunamis struck, or Haiti or New Orleans to see the devastation caused by hurricanes.
Global warming: the Alps to see the glaciers receding, or Siberia or Alaska to see buildings sinking as the permafrost melts, or the Amazon rainforest (start from Manaus, the region's capital) to see the forest being chopped down.

Travel there by *Google Earth*. You will be doing this without putting yourself in any danger. Find out more about the issues on *Wikipedia* and by using *Google*.

HOW TO HOLIDAY WITHOUT LEAVING YOUR ROOM

Instead of using your PC to have a holiday, use your imagination. Have a holiday without leaving your room. This is the ultimate in low-impact tourism, which 27-year old Frenchman Xavier De Maistre did in 1790. Read his classic travel book: *"A Journey Around My Room"*.

This may not be exciting enough for you. If you are short of ideas, check out the *Laboratory of Experimental Tourism*: **www.latourex.org**. Try *Chance Travel*, *Ero-Travel* or an *Expedition to K2*.

CREATE AN ALIBI FOR YOURSELF

You've had a virtual holiday, but you want to convince people that you've actually been there. Or you've told someone that you were going to go somewhere, but you didn't actually get there… or you went somewhere else instead. Then use the *Alibi Network* to provide evidence that you were where you said you were.

For example, you can show off by telling people that you went to the *World Economic Forum* and consorted with the world's top business leaders. The trouble was, that you weren't invited. Use *Alibi* to show that:

✳ You were booked to fly out to Davos. *Alibi* will provide an e-confirmation of your flight.

✳ You were in Davos. *Alibi* will give you a Davos telephone number, and switch the calls to your London telephone.

✳ You were staying at the Hotel Belvedere. *Alibi* will answer in the right accent, confirm you are staying there and provide documentary evidence such as receipts.

Use the *Alibi Network*: **http://alibinetwork.com**. Or if you can't afford that, then just visit the *World Economic Forum* website, and just talk as if you had been there: **www.weforum.org**

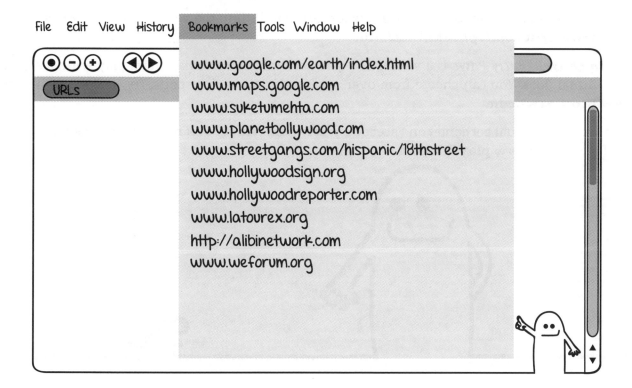

10. OWN A VIRTUAL PET

More living things on the planet means more resources being consumed and more carbon being emitted – all this will be contributing to global warming. Each pet has its own "Carbon Pawprint" based mostly on the food it eats.

Based on the land required to generate its food, a medium-sized dog has an annual footprint of 0.84 hectares – twice the 0.41 hectares required by a 4×4 driving 6,200 miles a year including the energy to build the car.

In their book *"Time to Eat the Dog?"*, authors Robert and Brenda Vale suggest that you downsize your pet… to a smaller pet, a vegetarian pet or even an edible pet. Think about having a hamster, a goldfish or a rabbit as a pet, rather than a large dog.

In a world threatened by global warming, you might decide to give up owning a pet altogether. But if you want or need a pet, then why not own a "Virtual Pet"?

YOUR VERY OWN VIRTUAL PET

Here are some good alternatives to owning a real-life pet, which provide you with something to look after and a friend in your life… and which generate zero emissions once you have acquired it:

* Get an electronic toy such as a *Tamagotchi*, which provides you with your own pet to feed, walk and look after.

* Adopt a virtual pet online.

* Join a virtual pet community, play games and enter into competitions with other virtual pet owners.

Cyberpets: Check out the following website for lots of links into the wonderful world of cyberpets: **www.virtualpet.com/vp/links/links.htm**

Best in show… *Furry Paws* is a virtual dog game where you can raise, train, play with, feed, and show virtual dogs. You can choose from over 190 breeds and 15 dog sports. Try it. Sign up. It's free! **www.furry-paws.com**

There are lots of virtual pet games on Facebook: **www.gamesfacebook.net/category.asp?cat=pet**
Play Pet Society: **www.playfish.com**

THE VIRTUAL PET PROJECT

Researchers at the *Massachusetts Institute of Technology* are collecting stories from virtual pet owners around the world. **http://web.mit.edu/sturkle/www/vpet.html**

These are some of the questions they are interested in:

1. What kinds of things do you and your pet do together?

2. Do you feel that you have a special relationship with it?

3. What do you like (and not like) about it?

4. What is it like to be a caretaker for a virtual pet?

5. How do friends, family members, and live pets react to your virtual pet and to you spending time with it?

6. Is your creature smart? Does it have feelings? Does it think? How do you know?

Send your answers by email to **virtualpets@mit.edu**

CHINA'S ONE-DOG POLICY

The Chinese authorities have just imposed a one-pet policy (which mirrors China's one-child policy). The officially-stated reason for this was to stop the rise of rabies. Dangerous and large dogs are also banned. Anyone keeping an unlicensed dog faces prosecution, and dog control officials will destroy surplus pets.

The one-child policy led to "Little Emperors" – children who were thoroughly spoiled by their parents and grandparents. The one-dog policy is also creating a similar phenomenon.

Pet Paradise opened in Beijing in February 2006. This doggie hotel is a posh version of a kennel. It has 30 private rooms each fitted with air-conditioning . The daily rate is US$10 per night – which is about the same as a cheap hotel room. Canines can watch cartoons on TV before their bedtime. Owner Liu Mingli explains, *"Chinese dogs are used to having television on at home in the evening."* The next plan is to build a swimming pool *for the dogs!*

AND WHAT ABOUT HAVING A PET POLAR BEAR?

Polar bears are at the frontline of global warming. As the Arctic ice melts, so their very existence will come under threat. *National Grid Floe* is a website created by the UK-US energy giant, which enables you to think about the plight of the polar bear, but also to take some simple actions to address global warming.

You sign up and give your polar bear a name. You are then asked some simple questions – for example *"Is it better to drink water from the tap or from a bottle kept in the fridge?"*. If you get the answer right, you get a chance to play with your bear and make it happy. At the same time, you can pledge to reduce your impact on the planet, which will do a little towards slowing Arctic warming. **www.nationalgridfloe.com**

Click2Change URLs
www.virtualpet.com/vp/links/links.htm
www.furry-paws.com
http://web.mit.edu/sturkle/www/vpet.html
virtualpets@mit.edu
www.nationalgridfloe.com
www.gamesfacebook.net/category.asp?cat=pet
www.playfish.com

11. COMMIT A RANDOM ACT

Instead of deciding what to do, leave it to chance. Do something completely unexpected – it might be a completely new experience, and you never know where it might lead. Use your computer to find out some random information that could inspire you. Or perhaps play dice to change the world!

GET IN THE MOOD

Access a random piece of information:

＊ Read a random *Wikipedia* encyclopaedia entry. If you don't like what comes up, try again: **http://en.wikipedia.org/wiki/Special:Random**

＊ Get some random information from the BBC's *"Guide to Life, the Universe and Everything"*: **www.h2g2.com/dna/h2g2/RandomEditedEntry**

Does this information interest you? Is it useful in any way? Does it spark off any ideas?

Generate a random number: Some so-called "random numbers" appear random, but are generated by a computer according to a formula. Others really are random; these are generated through a variety of techniques, including using atmospheric noise from a radio, or the emission of particles in radioactive decay, or the results of live keno games being played in real casinos. Generate a random number at: **www.random.org/nform.html**

Take a random walk: Take a break from your computer, and go for a walk.

Go out of your front door, turn first left, then first right, then second left, and knock on the third front door on the left-hand side of the road. Give the person who opens the door a copy of this book with your hope that they will do something for a better world. If nobody is in, continue walking. Give the book to the third person you see walking towards you.

Or just continue walking. Every time you come to a cross roads, flip a coin… if it's heads , you turn left; if tails, you turn right. See where chance will take you.

Write to a random lord in the British parliament's upper chamber: **www.writetothem.com/lords**

NOW DO SOMETHING RANDOM TO CHANGE THE WORLD

Compile a list of six problems and six possible actions to take in response to these. Make some of your actions easy, some more challenging. If you are stuck, use the list below.

Suggested problems, which are some of the "big issues" facing the world:

1. Human rights 2. Global warming
3. World poverty 4. Conflict and peace
5. Access to education 6. Global diseases

Then roll a first dice to choose which problem you will address. You might then want to do some research, to get facts about the issue, to find organisations which are dealing with it, to get ideas for what to do. Start with what you know already, and use *Wikpedia* and *Google*.

Suggested actions: ***Then roll a second dice which will tell you what to do.***

(1.) Petition the government. **http://epetitions.direct.gov.uk** tells you how. Get 100,000 signatures and your subject will be eligible for debate in Parliament.

(2.) Pledge to do something about the issue. Decide what, and use *PledgeBank* to get nine other people to do the same: **www.pledgebank.com**

(3.) Write a letter to the editor of your local newspaper.

(4.) E-mail everyone on your address book and post a message to all your *Facebook* friends.

(5.) Donate £25 to a charity to do something specific.

(6.) Raise money. Invite ten friends to dinner, asking each to contribute £10. Together choose a project to support.

COMMIT A RANDOM ACT OF KINDNESS

Think about the idea of giving freely to someone you meet at random.

For example, you go to the cinema, and you decide to pay not just for your own ticket, but also for the next person who turns up at the box office. You leave a card, saying that this is an act of generosity from a complete stranger… and you ask them do something for someone else and pass on the card. They might put a £5 note with the card next to an ATM machine. That person might buy a drink in a bar for someone… and the process continues creating a chain of happy people. Check out:

The Pay It Forward Movement: www.payitforwardmovement.org

Random Acts of Kindness: www.randomactsofkindness.org

Find out about Larry Stewart who became the *Secret Santa*: **www.secretsantausa.com**

The Extreme Kindness Tour was a three-month marathon to connect the world through kindness. In 2002, four friends set off in one motor-home to commit random acts of kindness in as many Canadian communities as they could manage. They knocked on doors offering to cook dinner, dragged office workers out for a game of hockey during the coffee break, and entertained kids at the children's hospital. They called themselves the *"Kindness Crew"*. Join them and connect the world through kindness. **http://extremekindness.com**

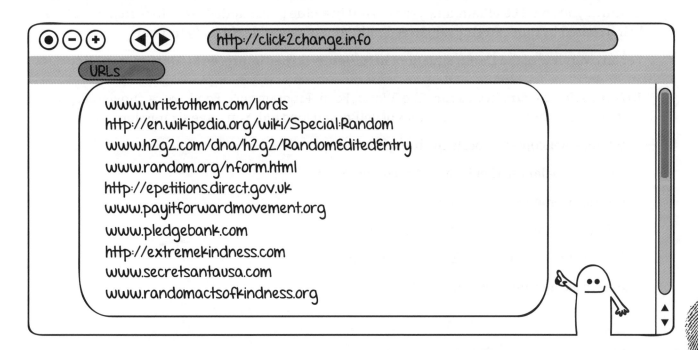

http://click2change.info

URLs

www.writetothem.com/lords
http://en.wikipedia.org/wiki/Special:Random
www.h2g2.com/dna/h2g2/RandomEditedEntry
www.random.org/nform.html
http://epetitions.direct.gov.uk
www.payitforwardmovement.org
www.pledgebank.com
http://extremekindness.com
www.secretsantausa.com
www.randomactsofkindness.org

12. PLAY GAMES TO CHANGE THE WORLD

Video and board games can educate as well as entertain. Listen to these two *TED Talks*:

www.ted.com/speakers/stuart_brown.html

www.ted.com/speakers/jane_mcgonigal.html

Many popular games involve zapping the enemy, and creating mayhem and destruction. There are also "games for good" which give you a better understanding of the world and some of its problems… and enable you to think about some of the solutions. Here are seven of the best. Have fun playing them.

1.   ***Learn the tactics of non-violence:*** *A Force More Powerful* teaches the tactics of non-violence. The game features ten scenarios inspired by recent history – conflicts against dictators, occupiers, colonisers, corrupt regimes, and struggles to secure political and human rights. Tactics include leafleting, protests, strikes, boycotts, mass action, civil disobedience and non-cooperation. **www. aforcemorepowerful.org**

   International Center on Nonviolent Conflict advocates non-violence to achieve social and political goals: **www.nonviolent-conflict.org**

   If you want to learn about warfare, play *America's Army* instead. This gives an insight into soldiering – from the barracks to the battlefield. **www.americasarmy.com**

2.   ***Become a Peace Maker:*** *PeaceMaker* is a one-player game where you take the role of either the Israeli Prime Minister or the Palestinian President. You react to events, from diplomatic negotiations to military attacks, and interact with eight other political leaders and social groups to try to create peace in the region. **www.peacemakergame.com**

   Mid-East Web provides access to resources on the Middle East: **www.mideastweb.org**

3.   ***Darfur is Dying:*** In Darfur in Western Sudan, genocide continues despite international concern. Each day civilians face the possibility of a mass killing, torture, rape having their village burnt to the ground and their property stolen. *Darfur is Dying* brings home the realities of daily life in Darfur… you could be Elham, a 14-year-old girl in a blue polka-dotted dress, in search of water and being chased by gun-carrying Janjaweed militiamen. **www.darfurisdying.com**

   For an overview of the Darfur situation: **http://en.wikipedia.org/wiki/Darfur_conflict**

4.   ***Bring relief to famine areas:*** The World Food Programme's *Food Force* shows people the problems of hunger and the difficulties of delivering food aid. You have six missions to complete:

   ✱ Pilot a helicopter to locate the hungry.

   ✱ Create a balanced diet for a feeding programme.

   ✱ Airdrop emergency food aid.

   ✱ Buy food and transport it to where it's needed.

   ✱ Guide the convoy of trucks to a feeding centre.

   ✱ Help a community rebuild itself.

Play *Food Force* at **www.wfp.org/how-to-help/individuals/food-force**

Explore hunger in the world: **www.wfp.org**

5. ***Do you have what it takes to be a Dictator?*** Are you ruthless enough to attain absolute power? You are Jomo Amin, rebel leader of the Southern Swamp. You currently have 40 soldiers and 30 rifles, 8,000 voters and 10,000 dollars. A famine is killing many people. Relief agencies want to transport the aid by through your province. Do you:

   1. Hijack the supply trucks and distribute the food amongst your own voters?
   2. Declare a cease-fire to allow the supplies to reach people in need?
   3. Refuse to allow the supplies through in order to weaken the President?

   Play *Banana Republic*: **www.benco-boardgames.com/bananarepublicgame.htm**

   Transparency International is a global network fighting corruption: **www.transparency.org**

6. ***Play games with the climate.*** Can global warming be controlled? The world has to balance economic interests and the needs of poor people in developing countries with ever-increasing global emissions. Hard decisions have to be made – whether to invest in exploiting sources of fossil fuel offsetting this by purchasing carbon credits or to create more expensive hi-tech green energy solutions. If nothing is done, then the Earth's average temperature might rise by 4°. Everyone would be the loser!

   Game makers have created games that explore the issues of climate action. Find out about climate games at **http://en.wikipedia.org/wiki/Global_warming_game**

   Play *World Without Oil* which simulates the beginning of a global oil crisis and inspires players to change their daily energy habits. **www.worldwithoutoil.org**

   Understand the impact of climate change. Mark Lynas wrote a book called *"Six Degrees"* which summarises the research into the impact of each one degree of the earth's temperature rise. His book will frighten you, and possibly stir you to action. **www.marklynas.org**

7. ***Come up with creative solutions to the world's most pressing social problems.*** Play the *World Bank Institute's Evoke* which is a 10-week crash course in changing the world designed especially for young people, 13 years and up. Top players earned online mentorships with experienced social innovators and business leaders from around the world, and scholarships to share their vision for the future at an Evoke Summit held in Washington DC. The game ran in March 2010. Sign up for the next season **www.urgentevoke.com**

www.aforcemorepowerful.org
www.ted.com/speakers/stuart_brown.html
www.ted.com/speakers/jane_mcgonigal.html
www.nonviolent-conflict.org
www.americasarmy.com
www.peacemakergame.com
www.mideastweb.org
www.darfurisdying.com
www.marklynas.org
www.worldwithoutoil.org

www.transparency.org
www.marklynas.org
www.worldwithoutoil.org
www.transparency.org
www.wfp.org
www.urgentevoke.com
www.wfp.org/how-to-help/individuals/food-force
http://en.wikipedia.org/wiki/Darfur_conflict
www.benco-boardgames.com/bananarepublicgame.htm
http://en.wikipedia.org/wiki/Global_warming_game

13. HAVE A SECOND LIFE

Second Life is a 3-D virtual world entirely built and owned by its residents. Over 18 million people from around the world have registered, and an average of 38,000 are logged on at any moment. *Second Life* is now being used for marketing fashion, film and music to real world residents. It could become an interesting playground for any social entrepreneur and for charity promotions.

Joining is free, but you need to be over 16. Your first step is to create an "Avatar" – a personification of the character that you want to be in *Second Life*. Decide who you are, your look, your personality and your role. This could be the person you are or who you've always wanted to be… glamorous, articulate, popular. Or you might choose to indulge your fantasies… perhaps as a beach bum or a lap dancer. The choice is yours.

Sign up as a *Premium Member* and you can acquire land and get other benefits. This costs $72 per year. You choose what you do with your land. You could rent it out or develop it, building: *"A dream home, or a thunderdome, a small shop or a gigantic shopping centre"*. Creating *"A dance club or a giant bathtub"*. Or *"Planting trees to construct a secluded retreat in the pristine virtual wilderness."*

You can also acquire *Linden Dollars*, the currency used in *Second Life*. You can do this officially at the *LindeX Currency Exchange*, with US$1 equalling around 260 Linden Dollars; but you can also exchange your money unofficially, the rate fluctuating with supply and demand.

BECOME A SECOND LIFE ENTREPRENEUR

Once you have *Second Life* money, you can start trading. You can buy, sell and even make a profit. You can convert any profit back into real money.

There are as many opportunities for innovation and enterprise in Second Life as there are in the real world. Here are a few examples of what people are doing:

party planner
casino operator
fashion designer
custom avatar designer
tour guide
musician
bodyguard
private detective
land speculator
landscape architect
publicist

NON-PROFITS AND SECOND LIFE

Many for-profit businesses have established a presence in *Second Life*, including *BMW*, *Toyota*, *Microsoft*, *Calvin Klein*, *Playboy*, *MTV*, *BBC Radio*, *The Weather Channel* and *Reuters*. Now it is the turn of non-profits.

Organisations such as the *Fund for Animal Welfare*, *Reporters Without Borders* and *Save the Children* have set up virtual branches in *Second Life* to promote their cause and garner support. Here are some examples:

✴ *America's Second Harvest* (A2H) took part in the grand opening of the *Second Life's* first supermarket, advertising its presence on billboards and posters.

✴ The *American Cancer Society* (ACS) runs a virtual version of its *Relay for Life* fund-raising event on *Second Life*. In 2010, this raised nearly $222,000: **http://wiki.secondlife.com/wiki/Relay_For_Life_of_Second_Life**

Second Life is a fantasy world. Many people's fantasies are to be strong, sexy, super-intelligent, athletic, successful, rich… But why not enter *Second Life* as a "saint" with the aim of changing this second world. You could try to become the *"Mother Theresa of Second Life"*. You could show the other residents that there is more to a *Second Life* than glamour, consumption and profit. Here are some ideas:

✴ Raise an issue such as global warming. Develop a Linden Dollar carbon offset scheme. Or encourage *Second Life* residents to live environmentally sustainable lives.

✴ Become a *Second Life* fundraiser. Persuade people to give, just as they might do in real life. Organise a fundraising event. Raise money in Linden Dollars, convert it into real Dollars and use this to address some real world problems.

Find out more: **http://secondlife.com**

Find out about non-profits in *Second Life*: **www.nonprofitcommons.org**

Build your own virtual world at *Active Worlds* and explore 1,000 others: **www.activeworlds.com**

AND WHAT ABOUT THE NEXT LIFE?

If having a second life doesn't appeal to you, why not think about the life hereafter? Why not do something to try to change the next world? Of course if you are a Hindu, you might just come back to this world reincarnated – perhaps as a termite or a krill, where opportunities for changing the world would be quite limited!

Here are a few things you could do in this life which might affect your prospects for the hereafter. You could wash away your sins with a special soap; or re-live the ten plagues with finger puppets; or suck a "Testamint"; or pray with a credit card rosary… For a bit of fun, go to and check out *Gadgets for God* at: **http://shipoffools.com**

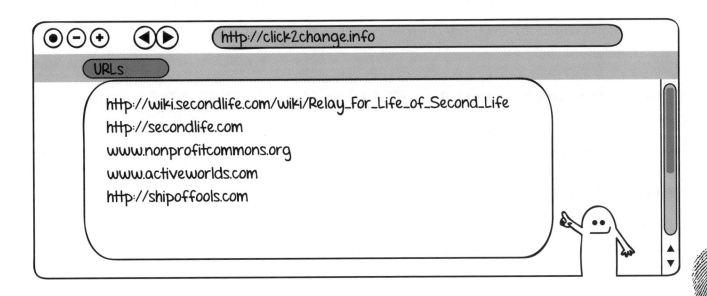

http://click2change.info

URLs

http://wiki.secondlife.com/wiki/Relay_For_Life_of_Second_Life
http://secondlife.com
www.nonprofitcommons.org
www.activeworlds.com
http://shipoffools.com

14. INVENT A CONSPIRACY THEORY

✳ Who killed John F Kennedy? Or Dr Martin Luther King Jr?

✳ Was Harold Wilson, British Prime Minister from 1964, a KGB agent?

✳ Was Slobodan Milosovic murdered whilst on trial in The Hague for war crimes?

✳ Did the Apollo Moon Landing ever take place? Or was it simulated on earth?

✳ Did UFOs land at Roswell? What really happened on that night in 1947?

✳ Did Paul McCartney die in 1966 to be replaced by a look-alike, with the clues hidden in Beatles songs and album cover artwork?

✳ Is global warming a fabrication by environmentalists to undermine Big Oil and the airline industry?

Sometimes the facts do not seem to be quite right. So we look for an alternative explanation. Occasionally the idea that there has been a conspiracy takes root and will just not go away – as in the case of JFK's assassination – because they just don't want us to know what actually happened. Or the truth might be too embarrassing to be revealed – it could have been more of a "cock-up" than a conspiracy.

So when something happens and you just don't believe what you are being told, think about the possibility that there might be a conspiracy to hide the truth. You could just be right!

For example, was the death of Diana Princess of Wales the accident that it was reported to be? Or was she murdered just before the news broke that she was expecting a child by Dodi Al-Fayed (and the likelihood that this child, a half-brother to a future British King, would be brought up a Muslim)? The idea of a conspiracy seemed to grow as the authorities continued to mishandle the case – from having a number of partial enquiries to suggesting that the inquest be heard by a single hand-picked judge rather than in front of a jury. And even if the "facts" in the end "prove" that the death was accidental, the idea that there was a conspiracy seems likely to persist.

Check out the following:

✳ The *Wikipedia* entry on conspiracy theories: **http://en.wikipedia.org/wiki/Conspiracy_theory**

✳ This website which is devoted to conspiracies and cover ups: **www.coverups.com**

✳ *"The Rough Guide to Conspiracy Theories"*, which is available from *Amazon*.

And...

✳ Find out the facts about the sighting of a UFO at Roswell:
http://en.wikipedia.org/wiki/Roswell_UFO_incident

✳ Google *"Diana Conspiracy Theory"*, and browse the nearly 5.3 million listed pages.

✳ Join the *Flat Earth Society*. They welcome both sceptics and believers: **http://theflatearthsociety.org**

INVENT A CONSPIRACY THEORY

Next time you are given an explanation that seems dubious or you think there is a motive for things being otherwise, then think *"Conspiracy"*. Create and circulate your own conspiracy theory.

* *Gather the facts.* See if you can get information that nobody else has. In the absence of facts, just surmise… maybe the facts will appear later and justify your case. Remember that facts are often stranger than fiction.

* *Be sceptical.* Question the official explanations.

* *Set up a website*, which you will make a focal point for disseminating your conspiracy theory.

* *Give your conspiracy theory legs.* Write letters, post messages in chatrooms and on blogs, contact the press, get interviewed. Spread the idea widely. See if you can get the idea to go around the world.

INVENT A RUMOUR

Snopes is a place to find out about urban legends, strange news stories, net lore, superstitions and folk wisdom. If you've ever wondered about alligators in sewers, HIV-loaded needles in theatre seats, $250 cookie recipes and much else, then go to **www.snopes.com**

BECOME A SKEPTIC (YES WITH A K NOT A C!)

The *Skeptics Society* is an organisation of scholars, scientists, historians, magicians, professors and teachers, and anyone curious about controversial ideas, extraordinary claims, revolutionary ideas, and the promotion of science. Their mission is to serve as an educational tool for those seeking clarification and views on controversial ideas and claims. **www.skeptic.com**

PLAY AN APRIL FOOLS JOKE

All Fools Day (otherwise known as April Fools Day) is a day to play practical jokes on friends and colleagues. *"April 1… the day upon which we are reminded of what we are on the other three-hundred and sixty-four."* – Mark Twain.

All about April Fool's Day: **http://en.wikipedia.org/wiki/April_Fool's_Day**

Top April Fool hoaxes of all time: **www.museumofhoaxes.com/hoax/aprilfool**

View the spaghetti harvest in Switzerland featured in the BBC's flagship documentary programme broadcast on 1st April 1957: **http://news.bbc.co.uk/onthisday** then go to *April 1*.

Find out more about *San Serriffe*, a fictitious island state which had a special supplement devoted to it in the *Guardian* newspaper on 1st April 1977: **http://en.wikipedia.org/wiki/San_Serriffe**

Click2Change URLs

http://en.wikipedia.org/wiki/Conspiracy_theory

www.coverups.com

http://en.wikipedia.org/wiki/Roswell_UFO_incident

http://theflatearthsociety.org

www.snopes.com

www.skeptic.com

http://en.wikipedia.org/wiki/April_Fool's_Day

www.museumofhoaxes.com/hoax/aprilfool

http://news.bbc.co.uk/onthisday

http://en.wikipedia.org/wiki/San_Serriffe

15. CLICK & DONATE

Here's a nifty way of giving money which won't cost you a penny. There are websites where your click on an icon will trigger a donation The money for this comes from the website's sponsors, who pay a small sum for each visitor to the website; this revenue pays for the donation with the remainder going to the website owner to pay for operating costs (and profits). Additional revenue is generated through the sale of merchandise.

The amount of money each click triggers is tiny, but it is real money which will make a real difference… and at no cost to you. So get into the habit of clicking and donating!

What you can do….

1. Go to a *Click & Donate* website and click on the icon to trigger a donation. If you do this once a day, it will multiply the impact 365 times over the course of a year. Some sites will send you a daily reminder.

2. Make the website the home page for your internet browser. When you turn on your computer and open up your browser, the icon will be there waiting to be clicked. After you have done that, you can get on with the rest of your day.

3. Use the internet home page rotating tool *What Page* so that a different page appears each time you go to your Home Page. This will enable you to click and donate on lots of pages during the course of the day (most *Click & Donate* websites only allow you to click once a day). **www.whatpage.org**

4. Get a techno-wizard to develop a start-up routine for your computer which automatically gets your computer to visit a sequence of *Click & Donate* websites and trigger a donation from each; then only after your computer has done this, will it go to your home page which will be your search engine of choice.

5. Tell all your friends. There is a facility on many of the sites to do this. Get them clicking too.

SET UP A CLICKERS GROUP

A *Clickers Group* is a small group of friends who together agree to click as often as they can on a particular website or several, and together try to reach a target for the amount they raise. For example, a group of footballers could agree together to save an area of the rainforest equal to the size of one football pitch – this would take a team of 11 people a little over a year to do. Or a group of children could each aim to feed one hungry child a day.

Members of the Clickers Group could meet together from time to time to celebrate their achievements, to discuss the issue or to plan a much more ambitious project. The Group could be linked together via a social networking site – such as *FaceBook*.

CLICK AND SAVE THE RAINFOREST

Originally there were 6 million square miles of tropical rainforest across the world. Today as a result of deforestation, only around one-third of this still remains; and the area continues to shrink rapidly. Almost two acres of rainforest disappear every second. This leads to soil erosion, loss of biodiversity and an increase in carbon dioxide in the atmosphere. Click on the *Rainforest Site* and save one square metre – that's about as much space as you take up sitting at your computer. **www.therainforestsite.com**

And then watch this moving film about Indonesian rainforest destruction: **www.greenthefilm.com**

DO SOMETHING ABOUT HUNGER IN THE WORLD

24,000 people die every day from hunger, and 75% of these deaths are children under the age of five. The majority of hunger deaths are caused by extreme poverty – famine and wars being the cause of just 10%. It can take just a few simple resources for impoverished people to grow enough food to become self-sufficient: this includes seeds, tools, access to water and improvements in farming techniques. Find out more about world poverty at **www.poverty.com**

The Hunger Site was launched in 1999. For each click you make on the icon, one cup of staple food is donated. **www.thehungersite.com**

At *FreeRice.com* you do an educational quiz. For every correct answer, 10 grains of rice are donated through the *World Food Programme*. Continue playing, and you will learn whilst also doing something about world hunger: **www.freerice.com**

SOME OTHER CLICK & DONATE SITES

The Ecology Fund: **http://ecologyfund.com**
The Child Health Site: **www.thechildhealthsite.com**
The Literacy Site: **www.theliteracysite.com**
Climb against Breast Cancer: **http://breastcancer.care2.com**
Race to Save Baby Seals: **http://babyseals.care2.com**

For an up-to-date list of *Click & Donate* websites go to: **http://distributedcomputing.info/ap-charity.html** and **www.charityclickdonation.com**

Click2Change URLs:
www.whatpage.org
www.therainforestsite.com
www.greenthefilm.com
www.poverty.com
www.thehungersite.com
www.freerice.com
http://ecologyfund.com
www.thechildhealthsite.com
www.theliteracysite.com
http://breastcancer.care2.com
http://babyseals.care2.com
http://distributedcomputing.info/ap-charity.html
www.charityclickdonation.com

16. SEARCH AND RAISE MONEY

The internet has become a huge marketplace where companies vie with each other to get people to visit their websites, and they are prepared to pay for this. On *Google* and other search sites, advertisers pay a few pennies when people click on text and image links which takes them to their website. This is now the fastest growing segment of the advertising industry.

A number of search services channel a proportion of this click-through revenue to charity. Some benefit a pre-selected list of charities. Others are for any charity – which can include yours if you register. The amount you receive will be based on the amount of clicking that is done by you and your supporters. Over a year and with lots of your supporters searching, the amount can be quite substantial. The more of your supporters you can persuade to do this, the more money you will raise.

If you want to benefit a cause you believe in, sign up and start searching. It will help change the world – and like *Click & Donate*, it won't cost you a penny.

In the USA
GoodSearch uses *Yahoo*; you can direct the money to any US non-profit or school. **www.goodsearch.com**

Search Kindly uses *Google*; it has a monthly charity selected by votes of visitors to the site. **http://searchkindly.org**

In the UK
The Environment Site uses Yahoo; funds raised go to a specified environmental charity. **www.theenvironmentsite.org/search.php**

Everyclick uses *Ask*; a charity signs up and receives 50% of the income from searches made by its supporters. If a searcher does not choose a specific charity, the money is divided up between all charities on *Everyclick*. **www.everyclick.com**

Magic Taxi uses *Yahoo*; it gives 50% of net revenue to 18 UK charities. Your search benefits a daily featured charity, or you can choose from amongst the 18. **www.magictaxi.com**

If each search generates around one US Cent for charity, and each supporter clicks on an ad twice a day then:
> 100 supporters doing this will raise $730 per annum.
> 1,000 supporters will raise $7,300 per annum.
> 10,000 supporters will raise $73,000 per annum.

THE POWER OF GOOGLE

Google started in 1998 as a youthful alternative to the search engines run by established IT companies. In just a few years, it has become the major player on the web. Its mission statement is "*To organise the world's information and make it universally accessible and useful*". And its slogan is "*Don't be evil*".

Google's revenue comes largely from advertising. *AdWords* enables advertisers to display advertisements in *Google*'s search results and the *Google Content Network*, either on a cost-per-click or a cost-per-view basis. *Adsense* enables other websites to display an advertisement on their own site, and earn money every time it is clicked.

Here are some Google websites:
Google Guide: a guide to using *Google* effectively: **www.googleguide.com**

Google Weblog: An unofficial blog about *Google*: **http://google.blogspace.com**

GoogleWatch: As *Google*'s power and influence grow, this website reports on the public interest issues that this raises. **www.google-watch.org**

Scroogle: A way of *Googling* developed by *GoogleWatch* so that the search cannot traced back to your internet address: **www.scroogle.org**

Elgoog: This is *"Google"* spelt backwards; this mirror image of *Google* displays all text in reverse. Though originally created for fun, it can be used to avoid internet censorship. **http://elgoog.rb-hosting.de**

GoogleWhack: Enter two words of between 4 and 30 characters and search on *Google*. You get a *"GoogleWhack"* if the search produces just one result. **www.googlewhack.com**

Googawho: allows you to search on *Google* and another search engine with the results displayed side by side. **www.googawho.com**

SEARCH IN THE DARK

Blackle saves energy because the screen is reversed, so that the background is black and the text is white. Your monitor requires less power to display a predominantly black (or dark) screen than a white (or light) screen. *Blackle* users have saved over 2.7 million watt-hours. **www.blackle.com**. *Blackle* energy-saving tips are at: **www.blackle.com/tips**

You can also search in colour if your life needs brightening up. Choose a colour including pink, purple, green, rainbow at: **www.searchincolor.net** or at **www.thinkpinksearch.com**. Or try **http://googlepink.co.uk**

Earth Hour started in Australia in March 2007. People were asked to switch off their electricity for one hour. By 2010, the idea had spread around the world with over 5,000 cities in 128 countries participating. In 2008, Google celebrated *Earth Hour* by reversing out its screen and telling visitors *"We've turned the lights out. Now it's your turn."* Find out about the next *Earth Hour* at: **www.earthhour.org**

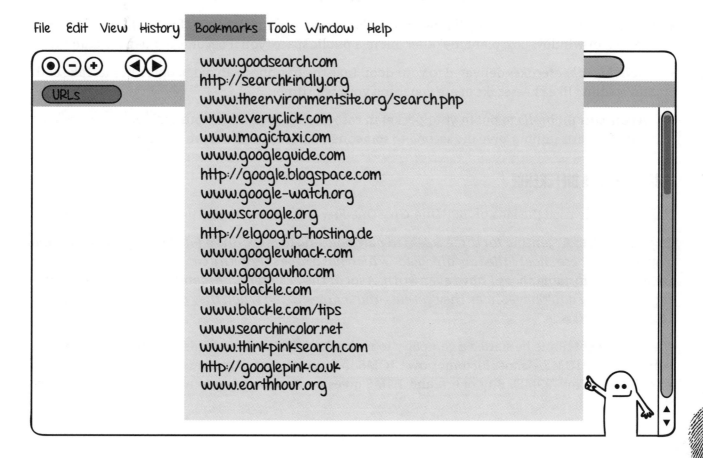

File   Edit   View   History   Bookmarks   Tools   Window   Help

URLs

www.goodsearch.com
http://searchkindly.org
www.theenvironmentsite.org/search.php
www.everyclick.com
www.magictaxi.com
www.googleguide.com
http://google.blogspace.com
www.google-watch.org
www.scroogle.org
http://elgoog.rb-hosting.de
www.googlewhack.com
www.googawho.com
www.blackle.com
www.blackle.com/tips
www.searchincolor.net
www.thinkpinksearch.com
http://googlepink.co.uk
www.earthhour.org

17. BUY ONE, GIVE ONE FREE

The word *"BOGOF"* stands for *"Buy One, Get One Free"*? This is an increasingly common and highly effective form of sales promotion. People like getting something for free. Next time there's a BOGOF special offer, why not buy one for yourself, but donate the free second item to someone who needs it? This will make you feel good, and your donation will have effectively cost you nothing.

Buy One, *GIVE* One Free could become the new form of giving. It could become a movement that creates philanthropy out of consumerism. Get started on your desktop. Search for something you want that's on a BOGOF offer, buy it online and then give the second item away.

GET GIVING

You'll find all sorts of things available to *"Buy One Get One Free"*. Just type these words into *Google*, and limit the search to pages from your own country. See what comes up.

At the time of writing, you could have chosen from 239,000 UK pages of BOGOFs! Here are some examples of what you could have done:

✳ *Mountainwear* to keep you warm (fleeces and t-shirts). Buy one, give the other to someone sleeping rough. It can get cold outdoors at night, even in summer.

✳ *Cast iron casseroles* (one free 16cm casserole with every 22cm casserole purchased). Buy one for yourself, give the other to a women's refuge.

✳ A *"Red Letter Day at a Spa"*, where you bring a guest for free. Book to have 7 hours of bliss and take someone from the women's refuge with you. She'll have an uplifting experience.

✳ *Crocosmia "Norwich Canary" bulbs*, which bloom with beautiful yellow flowers. Buy one for your garden or window box; plant the other out in a public space (you'll become a "guerrilla gardener").

✳ *Delicious cheesecakes* delivered to your door. Take the free one to an old people's home. Take both if you don't like cheesecake or are watching your waistline.

✳ A *compact umbrella* to put in your pocket in case it rains. Take them both with you when you go out. If it starts raining, give the second to someone who looks as if they're going to get really wet.

SHOES MAKING A DIFFERENCE

Blake Mycoskie used the idea of *"Buy One, Give One Free"* for selling shoes. This is how he got started:

"I went down to Argentina for three weeks to play polo and to relax, and a lot of the farmers and polo players wore these shoes called an "alpagata" which has a rope sole with a cardboard interior. They are the most comfortable shoes I have ever worn. A lot of the children in Argentina don't have shoes... and when they don't have shoes, they get cuts and scrapes... and when they get infected, it turns into a bigger health issue."

When Blake got home he started a company to make shoes adapted from this Argentinian design. He called his shoe *TOMS* – "shoes for tomorrow". TOMS shoes cost $44 and upwards a pair ($34 and upwards for children's Tiny TOMS). Buy one... and TOMS gives another pair free to a child in need in a poor country. In 2006, Blake distributed 10,000 pairs of shoes. By September 2010, over 1 million pairs had been given away. **www.toms.com**

Style your sole: Organise a "style your own party" where your friends decorate their own pairs of TOMS, using spray paint, chalk, ink pens, sharpies, fabric paint, stencils, glitter, fabric, thread…
What you do is:

1. *Fix a date*. Make this a few weeks ahead, so the shoes have time to arrive.

2. *Draw up an invite list*, and send out the invitations. Ask people to tell you their shoe size when they reply.

3. *Collect money* from your guests for their shoes.

4. *Place your order* for white TOMS.

5. *Hold the party*. Have fun with your friends.

6. *Upload the most wacky designs* to the *StyleYourSole* website

www.toms.com/style-your-sole

Go shoeless for a day: Wake up without shoes. Walk without shoes. Work without shoes. Dance without shoes. Help raise awareness of the impact that a pair of shoes can have on a child's life by going shoeless for one day in April. Over 250,000 people did this in 2010 and over 1,600 events were organised around the world. **www.onedaywithoutshoes.com**

BUY NOTHING

Instead of buying, don't go shopping, Reduce your impact on the planet. Buy nothing today.

Buy nothing on *Buy Nothing Day*: **www.buynothingday.co.uk** and
www.ecoplan.org/ibnd/ib_index.htm

Buy nothing for *Buy Nothing Christmas*. **www.buynothingchristmas.org**

New Message ⊖ ▣ ⊗

File   Edit   View   Insert   Format   Tools   Message   Help

✉→
Send

From: click2change@gmail.com

To:

Cc:

Subject: URLs

www.toms.com
www.toms.com/style-your-sole
www.onedaywithoutshoes.com
www.buynothingday.co.uk
www.ecoplan.org/ibnd/ib_index.htm
www.buynothingchristmas.org

18. GIVE YOURSELF AWAY

In 2001, conceptual artist Michael Landy destroyed everything he possessed. In a vacant shop in London's Oxford Street he systematically shredded his clothes, his personal effects, his furniture and pictures, his kitchen equipment, his passport and birth certificate… in fact, everything. What we are asking you to do is a little bit easier and a lot more comfortable. We want you to give yourself away. All of you. Your body, your organs, your blood, even your hair. Get online right now, and start organising this.

DONATE YOUR BODY

Are you dying to go to medical school? But perhaps the exams are too hard and you can't manage the grades. Or maybe you've set your hopes on a completely different and much more fulfilling career. Or you are too old…

Here's a really easy way to get into a medical school without the bother of studying to become a doctor. Medical schools need bodies to help teach their students the principles of anatomy; they need brains for altzheimers research. If you want to donate your body or your brain, here's what to do:

1. Contact a hospital (or medical school) and tell them you plan to donate your body to them. Go to their website as a first step.

2. Put your request in writing. Sign and date the letter, and get it witnessed. Tell your friends and family. They are then legally obliged to hand over the body after your death.

3. Next you must die!

4. Immediately your death has been registered, your executors should hand over your body to your chosen hospital.

5. The hospital will assess whether they can use your body. Only bodies that are intact and disease free are accepted.

6. Your body is then embalmed and frozen within three days of death. It can be used for up to three years.

7. Around four medical students will work on your body, dissecting first an arm and a leg, then the head and the neck, and so on until they've finished with you.

8. Finally your body is returned to your family for burial or cremation.

You won't feel a thing. That's a promise! And don't be embarrassed. You won't be recognisable, as the embalming turns you a colourless grey – something like pumice stone.

National: **www.hta.gov.uk/bodyorganandtissuedonation/howtodonateyourbody.cfm**
London: **www.rcseng.ac.uk/education/donate-your-body-to-medical-science**

Donate your body (but only in Tennessee) to study decomposition, and then for study of skeletons: **www.uthsc.edu/anatomy-neurobiology/files/DonorFAQ.pdf**

DONATE YOUR ORGANS

More than 5,500 people in the UK are waiting for an organ transplant that could save or dramatically improve their life. Most need a kidney; others want a heart, a lung or a liver. Nearly 400 people die each year whilst waiting for a transplant.

Donate your organs to help keep someone else alive after your death. The person in possession of your body at the time of your death (your executor) has to be willing to donate your organs and should have no reason to believe you would not have wished this. You can express your wishes by putting your name on the *Organ Donor Register* and having an *Organ Donor Card*.

Organs that can be donated include:

Brain	Heart
Lungs	Kidneys
Pancreas	Liver
Small bowel	

Tissues that can be donated include:

Corneas	Skin
Bone	Heart valves

Take the first step right now. Register online as an organ donor at: **www.uktransplant.org.uk**

GIVE BLOOD

You can't do this online. Just show up at a blood donor centre. You will be asked some questions about your health and lifestyle to make sure you've not been exposed to an infection that could be passed on – such as hepatitis, HIV, malaria and Creutzfeldt Jakob Disease (CJD).

If you're OK, a drop of blood is taken from your finger and tested to make sure you're not anaemic. Then just under a pint of your blood is taken. The procedure takes ten minutes. Contact the *National Blood Service (UK)*: **www.blood.co.uk**

DONATE YOUR HAIR

Your hair can be made into hairpieces for children suffering medical hair loss through Alopecia Aresta or as cancer patients undergoing chemotherapy. The wigs are made to order, which takes up to two months. Donate your hair to *Locks of Love* from anywhere in the world. You need a minimum 25cms hair length. **www.locksoflove.org**

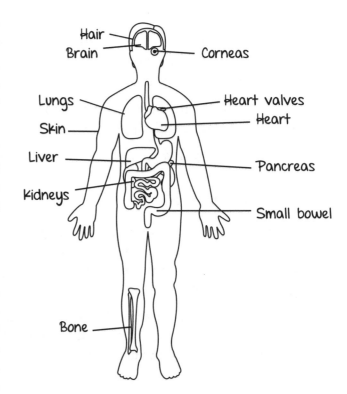

And while you are about it... Donate your old spectacles to people in the developing world through *Vision Aid Overseas*. You just take them to an optician: **www.vao.org.uk**

www.hta.gov.uk/bodyorganandtissuedonation/howtodonateyourbody.cfm
www.rcseng.ac.uk/education/donate-your-body-to-medical-science
www.uthsc.edu/anatomy-neurobiology/files/DonorFAQ.pdf
www.uktransplant.org.uk
www.blood.co.uk
www.locksoflove.org
www.vao.org.uk

19. GET RID OF ALL YOUR UNWANTED STUFF

We live in a consumer society. Through special offers, clever brand marketing, in-your-face advertising and celebrity endorsements, we are encouraged to purchase far more than we actually need. When fashion changes, we buy something new. What was perfectly good is shoved to the back of the cupboard. We also have things which we once needed, such as children's toys; our kids grow up, so we have cupboards full of stuff that's no longer used. Then there are the books we have read, which are put on a shelf to gather dust.

You may not be aware of how much stuff you have accumulated. It will probably be much more than you think. So why not do something about it.

Start by going through all your possessions to see what you really need and want to keep. Adopt the motto *"If in doubt, throw it out"*. Make a pile of your no-longer-needed possessions and tweet a photograph of this to your friends.

Instead of throwing the stuff out, find someone who would like it. Here are two ideas for doing this:

✳ *Freecycle* it… and support the ideals of a cooperative, sharing society.

✳ Auction it on *eBay*… then donate the proceeds to changing the world.

BECOME A FREECYCLER

Your local *Freecycling* group enables you to advertise something on its website and find another member of the group who wants it. Or if you need something, you might find it on *Freecycle*. There is just one rule – everything must be free. Freely given, free to get. Non-profit groups as well as individuals can *Freecycle*.

There are now 5,000 *Freecycling* groups around the world with a total of 8.4 million members. Most groups have hundreds and some thousands of members. Check to see if there is a group in your area. If there is, join it and use it. If there isn't, why not start one? The *Freecycle* website tells you how in its *Moderator Manual*.

If you don't want to *Freecycle* or nobody wants your stuff, then take it to a charity shop, where someone will pay for it; and the proceeds go to charity. If the charity shop won't take it, then put it in the recycling bin.

Freecycle: **http://freecycle.org**

SELL IT ON EBAY

eBay was created in 1995 as an online marketplace for buying and selling. It now has over 100 million active users in some 30 countries. On any given day, many millions of items are on sale across thousands of categories, including antiques, toys, books, computers, sports, photography, electronics.

You can sell almost anything on *eBay* – including promises, such as having dinner with a celebrity, as well as actual things. These are some of the banned or restricted categories:

Tobacco, alcohol (although wine is allowed).

Drugs, drug paraphernalia.

Nazi paraphernalia.

Pirate recordings.
Military hardware, firearms, ammunition, explosives.
Used underwear, dirty used clothing.
Human parts and remains.
Live animals (with certain exceptions).
Lottery tickets, other gambling items.

Register as an eBay user: **www.ebay.co.uk**

If you are not already an *eBay* addict, there are some good guidebooks to *eBay*. Try Googling *"eBay Guide"* for up-to-date information. And see: **www.ebayhacks.com**

There is an *eBay* charity page where UK non-profits can publicise their *eBay* auctions. Why not set up an auction page for members of a local charity or community group to raise money? **http://pages.ebay.co.uk/ebayforcharity**

SOME UNUSUAL ITEMS SOLD ON EBAY

✳ Water said to have been left in a cup Elvis Presley once drank from was sold for $455.

✳ A Coventry University student sold a single cornflake for £1.20.

✳ Glastonbury mud from a muddy festival sold for an amazing £490

✳ A group of four men from Australia auctioned themselves to spend the weekend with, with the promise of *"beers, snags, good conversation and a hell of a lot of laughs"* for AU$1,300

✳ In April 2004, American entrepreneur Matt Rouse sold the right to choose a new middle name for himself. After receiving an $8,000 *"Buy It Now"* bid, the Utah courts refused to allow the name change.

HOW EBAY WAS FOUNDED

eBay was founded in 1995 by Pierre Omidyar when he was in his twenties. He wanted to create an efficient internet space for individuals and small businesses to trade. The very first item sold was a broken laser pointer which fetched $14.83. An astonished Omidyar contacted the winning bidder and asked if he understood that the laser pointer was broken. The buyer explained: *"I'm a collector of broken laser pointers"*. Pierre and Jeff Skoll who was hired as eBay's first President are now major philanthropists who support social entrepreneurship. Omidyar Network: **www.omidyar.net** and Skoll Foundation: **www.skollfoundation.org**

Click2Change URLs

http://freecycle.org
www.ebay.co.uk
www.ebayhacks.com
http://pages.ebay.co.uk/ebayforcharity
www.omidyar.net
www.skollfoundation.org

20. GIVE YOUR MONEY AWAY

You've clicked and searched… and donated without paying a penny *(15 and 16)*; bought one for yourself and given away one free *(17)*; given away all of yourself – your blood, your organs, your hair, and even your whole body *(18)*; freecycled and recycled everything you don't need *(19)*. What next?

In 1789, Benjamin Franklin wrote: *"In this world nothing can be said to be certain, except death and taxes"*. This is as true today as it was then – except that nowadays life expectancy is a lot longer and taxes a lot higher.

So why save all your money which will be taxed heavily when you die? Why not give more of it away during your lifetime, putting it to good use in changing the world and making other people's lives better?

In the end, this is a matter of personal choice. You can choose to give a bit more… and take pride in what this helps achieve. You'll probably find that donating £20 to give a "gift of sight" to a blind child gives you much more pleasure than going out for another half-good meal in a local diner.

Here are some things to do right now:

1. ***Decide to give away a proportion of your income.*** A tithe is 10%. Calculate how much this would be per annum, month, week or day at: **www.anycalculator.com/tithecalculator.htm**. How about giving 1% for starters? Or 0.7%, which is the UN recommended level for international aid? Or donate one day's pay, which is about 0.4% of your income. *Giving What We Can* encourages people to make a public pledge to give a substantial portion of their income (10% and upwards) to fighting global poverty, just a fraction of your income to make a big difference. **www.giving-whatwecan.org**

2. ***Donate your spare change.*** Each night before you go to bed, empty your pockets – all your coins, or just smaller denominations. Put them in a large glass jar. You will be surprised at how quickly the jar fills up. When it's full take it to the bank. Use this money as your "charity pot". You can also collect spare change electronically on *Ploink*. Choose up to three charities, click on the coin you want to donate. When you have collected more than £1, you pay the donation by credit card. **www.ploink.co.uk**

3. ***Donate fees*** you get for things such as public speaking or training.

4. ***Get a part-time job specifically to earn money for charity.*** You could babysit, work as a bartender, mow someone's lawn, wash their car. If people know you are doing this for charity, they might even pay you a bit more. And there's *Mechanical Turk*, where you can find small tasks to do on line… and then you get paid to do them: **www.mturk.com** Or try *Gigwalking* (in the USA only for now) using your mobile phone to earn money and *"Streetcred"*: **http://gigwalk.com**

5. ***Donate a part of any inheritance*** you receive.

6. ***Donate your surplus income***, everything in excess of what you actually need to live at the standard you want (assuming you are earning more than you need).

Get a credit card and open a *PayPal account* or a *CAF account* for online giving: **www.paypal.com** and **www.cafonline.org**. Next decide how much you want to give – and pledge to do this. Write a letter to yourself with your pledge. Sign it. Keep it in a safe place. It will act as a reminder.

What you give to is entirely up to you to decide. You could:

✳ Support something quite specific – and enjoy helping make that happen.

✳ If you are passionate about a cause, support that.

✳ Do some internet research or visit an online giving website to get ideas.

SOME INTERESTING ONLINE GIVING WEBSITES

Give India: lots of projects, many with several options for giving. You might end up building a well, sponsoring a child's education, providing eye operations… **www.giveindia.org**

Global Giving: a marketplace for high impact social and economic development projects around the world: **www.globalgiving.org**

Lit Liberation: Raising money for education in the USA and the developing world through monthly million dollar challenges, with monthly prizes for spreading the word and getting your friends to give: **http://litliberation.wordpress.com**

See the difference: If you could see the project and meet the people involved, this would encourage you to give. See videos which show the difference you could make with your money: **www.seethedifference.org**

And here are three websites to keep you up to date on fundraising ideas: **http://philanthropy.blogspot.com**, **http://givinginadigitalworld.org** and **www.sofii.org**

SOME INTRIGUING WAYS OF GIVING

Help build the Darfur Wall: The *Darfur Wall* is a grid of the numbers 1 to 400,000, each representing someone killed in Darfur. By donating $1 you light up your chosen number or a randomly generated number, turning it from grey to brilliant white. Proceeds go to four organisations working in Darfur. **http://darfurwall.org**

Light a candle for AIDS: The *Global Health Council* invites you to light a virtual candle as a memorial for anyone anywhere in the world who has been touched by HIV/AIDS. Do this, and then find an AIDS charity to donate to. **www.candlelightmemorial.org/light_candle**

Plant a sunflower for peace and prosperity: On 4th June 1996, the Defence Ministers of the USA, Russia and Ukraine met at the Pervomaisk missile base to celebrate Ukraine's transfer of its nuclear warheads to Russia for dismantling. The Ministers planted sunflowers where missiles were once buried. The *Sunflower Project* celebrates this gesture for peace by encouraging people everywhere to plant sunflowers in their gardens, on waste land or wherever. **www.sunflowerproject.com**. Do this. Then make a donation for peace. Here's one suggestion: **www.peacedirect.org**

PARTICIPATE IN A FUN EVENT

A good way of raising money is to participate in a fundraising event – anything from a Marathon or Triathlon to a fun run or a knit-in. You could do an hour in the local park or a fortnight walking the Great Wall of China. If you ask your friends to support you and your efforts to complete your challenge, you'll find that you can raise quite a lot.

Google *"Sponsored Events"* to find out more. Find an event that appeals to you. Many charities publicise their events on their website. Sign up and start asking your friends to sponsor you. Create a fundraising page on *Just Giving*: **www.justgiving.com**

DONATE A TWOLLAR

Twollars are a virtual currency for giving through *Twitter*. You can donate them to charity. Or you can give them to friends as mark of appreciation for something they have done or for just being who they are. For example, You might want to give Twollars when someone helps you by tweeting useful information, shares a tip, writes an inspiring Tweet or if you are just feeling generous.

Besides giving them to people, you can tweet your Twollars to a good cause. You can only support charities registered on the Twollars website. They then ask their supporters to buy these donated Twollars for real money. Everyone on Twitter has a starting balance of 50 Twollars. You can buy more at the rate of 10 Twollars = $1. This might become a fun way of giving money for good causes.
http://twollars.com

ASK OTHERS TO GIVE

You've done all you can with your own resources. Now's a good time to persuade others to follow your example and give their money away – either to the causes you are supporting, or to the things that concern them. Try doing these:

* *Telephone or email one person today* to ask them to support something you've supported. Tomorrow ask someone else. You may find this hard to do to start with, but you'll get used to it as you ask more people, and you'll get better over time.

* *When you go out shopping talk to the person behind you* in the checkout queue about the project you are passionate about. If they seem interested, ask them to support it.

* *Do an "Elevator Pitch"* the next time you are in a tall building going up (or down) in the lift. Tell everyone about your project in 4 quick sentences and ask them to support it.

GIVE WITH OTHER PEOPLE

You could pool your giving with other people, which will create a bigger fund to distribute, and you will all get the pleasure of doing something together. Here are some ideas:

* **Create a family fund**… yes, even your children can contribute some of their pocket money. Each month ask everyone to come up with a suggestion for what to support, then collectively decide which to give to and how much to give for that month.

* **Set up a giving circle** at work or with ten friends, each contributing a small percentage of their income. Set up a CAF charity account to obtain *Gift Aid* tax relief: **www.cafonline.org** Everyone can look out for interesting projects. Meet monthly to decide what to support.

* **Join The Funding Network**. This meets several times a year to hear interesting projects pitch for support. Members donate at a pledging session. This started in London, and is spreading to other cities in the UK and around the world. **www.thefundingnetwork.org.uk**

THE 100 FRIENDS PROJECT

"I am Marc Gold. I started the 100 Friends project in 1989. The idea is simple. Every year about 100 people contribute, and I take the money to Third World Countries and look for the neediest people I can find. I then put the money to work in the most compassionate, appropriate, culturally compatible, constructive and practical manner possible. I pay for my own travel expenses."

Over the years, Marc has helped build schools, drill wells, develop various livelihood projects, provide medicines and malaria nets in many countries. The amount collected and distributed year-on-year has grown. In 1992, it was just $2,111; in 2010, over $100,000.

Marc's *100 Friends* project is an exciting way of travelling the world (or indeed around your own country) whilst providing aid direct with the help of your friends. Become one of Marc's friends. Or start your own *100 Friends* group. **www.100friends.org**

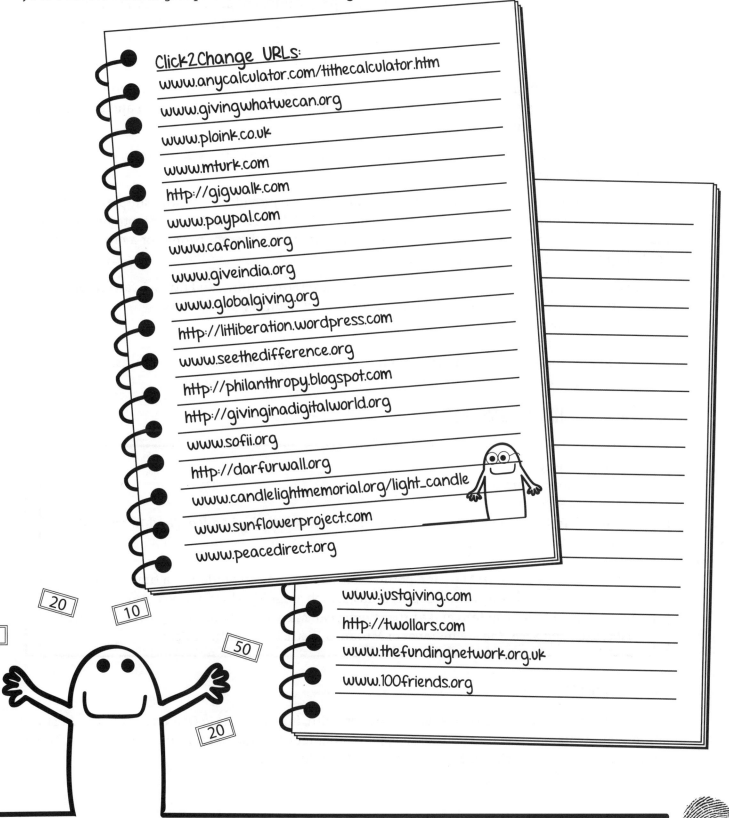

Click2Change URLs:

www.anycalculator.com/tithecalculator.htm

www.givingwhatwecan.org

www.ploink.co.uk

www.mturk.com

http://gigwalk.com

www.paypal.com

www.cafonline.org

www.giveindia.org

www.globalgiving.org

http://litliberation.wordpress.com

www.seethedifference.org

http://philanthropy.blogspot.com

http://givinginadigitalworld.org

www.sofii.org

http://darfurwall.org

www.candlelightmemorial.org/light_candle

www.sunflowerproject.com

www.peacedirect.org

www.justgiving.com

http://twollars.com

www.thefundingnetwork.org.uk

www.100friends.org

21. MAKE A LOAN, CHANGE A LIFE

The internet can create channels for giving that link people much more closely with what they decide to support. For the price of a dinner out, you could help a poor person somewhere in the developing world start or expand a micro-business and help them escape from poverty? You will not be giving to charity; you will be investing. If they make a success of their business, as most do, they will repay you.

You can do this through *Kiva* by credit card or *PayPal*. Typically an entrepreneur will need a few hundred dollars (the average is around $380). They will be selected, given training and advised by a local micro-finance institution.

Kiva started in 2005. By 2011, it had loaned $207million to 535,500 entrepreneurs in 59 countries with money lent by 575,000 investors.

"Kiva" is a Swahili word which means "unity" or "agreement. It provides you with a simple and effective way of making a difference to one person's and one family's life. The minimum investment is $25; the maximum, all they need. You could do a "portfolio" of loans to different people, or a group of friends could together sponsor one entrepreneur.

The more you lend, the bigger the difference you will make! So go online, and invest in an entrepreneur.
Step 1: Browse the *Kiva* website to choose a micro-entrepreneur: **www.kiva.org**
Step 2: Decide how much to lend.
Step 3: Make the loan.
Step 3: Receive progress reports whilst it is being repaid (typically within 6 to 12 months).
Step 4: When it is repaid, choose either to withdraw your money or to re-lend it.

AN EXAMPLE OF SOMEONE YOU COULD LEND TO

Location: Kenya.
Activity: Agriculture.
Loan needed: $900.
Loan use: To buy 500 day-old chicks, two dairy goats and chicken feed, and to renovate a chicken house.
Term: 10-18 months.
About the entrepreneur: Mary is a poultry farmer, rearing 200 broilers at a time, which are sold at $2.80. She also grows maize and beans, which are sold to local schools and her neighbours. Mary has been able to make profit every year. Mary has repaid three previous loans of $300, $500 and $700. She is a member of Muranga District Agricultural Board.

JOIN A KIVA GROUP

You can join a group of people you share an interest with, from atheists to Obama supporters, Australians or your workmates, so that you connect with other lenders and make an impact as a team. There are 15,000 *Kiva* groups to choose from. Or you can start your own.

SEE THE WORLD WITH KIVA

You can apply to become a *Kiva Fellow* which offers the opportunity to work directly with a Micro-Finance Institution and witness at first-hand the impact of microfinance; you pay your own travel and living expenses.

AND NOW THERE'S...

Like all good ideas, Kiva was bound to be copied. Here are two websites doing something similar but in different ways:

MyC4 enables you to invest your money in African entrepreneurs and receive interest on your investment. To find somebody to lend to, sort by status, industry, country, amount, wanted, interest rate, etc. Then read about the businesses you are interested in. When you have found someone you want to invest in, click the "*Invest*" button and type in the amount you want to lend and your required interest rate. If other people are prepared to lend at lower rates, then their bids will take precedence over yours. The process is a form of Dutch Auction. If your bid is no longer competitive, you will exit the auction. You will be notified by e-mail, and have the opportunity to enter a new bid at a lower rate. **www.myc4.com**

MicroPlace, owned by *eBay*, enables you to invest $100 or more in a micro-credit development agency which they lend onwards to micro-entrepreneurs. You choose the region and country you would like to invest in, and then choose an agency, the term of your loan (normally from 3 to 5 years) and the return you will get (normally ranging from 1.5% to 3% per annum). Unlike *Kiva*, you are not investing in any one individual or family, although you will find stories of some of the people your chosen agency has been able to help, which will give you a picture of the impact of your loan. **www.microplace.com**

And here are four websites which work in a similar way to *Kiva*:
Babyloan, based in France: **www.babyloan.org/en**
Rangde and *Milaap*, making microloans in India: **www.rangde.org** and **www.milaap.org**
Wokai, making microloans in China: **www.wokai.org**

Click2Change URLs

www.kiva.org
www.myc4.com
www.microplace.com
www.babyloan.org/en
www.rangde.org
www.milaap.org
www.wokai.org

22. KICKSTART A VENTURE

Instead of making a donation to a good cause, why not *invest* your money in a social venture? Help make something happen *and* get a return for your money. The process goes something like this.

1. A person *needs to raise money* for a project.

2. You *agree to support it.*

3. You *contribute money* (usually a small sum), which is only used when enough has been raised to get the project going (otherwise it's returned to you).

4. You are offered *something back* (it is a two-way transaction, not a gift).

5. You are *thanked twice* (first when you pay up, and then when enough has been collected for the project to proceed).

6. The project *goes ahead.*

7. You receive *progress reports*… and when the project's completed, you know exactly what has been achieved with your money.

8. You get the *benefits* that you were promised.

This technique is called "Crowdfunding", which aggregates relatively small sums from large numbers of people. The benefits they receive depend on how much people give. They are usually relevant, upbeat and fun, and might include:

* A share of any revenue generated by the venture.

* Your money back, if you gave it as a loan.

* Products created by the venture (books, CDs, DVDs).

* Invitations to special events.

* Opportunities that "money can't buy", such as dinner with a celebrity.

This book, for example, was crowdfunded. The benefits to the 250 people who put up the money to make it happen included free copies of the book, an invitation to a pedal-powered film screening, and a tandem tour with the author to see social enterprise at work.

As a crowdfunder, you are not simply a supporter. The idea is that become part of "a crowd of people" around the venture, who *together* are making something useful happen. You may also find that you are able to contribute in other ways to the success of the venture, such as finding others who would like to invest in it, or offering ideas and your contacts to help it succeed.

THE AGE OF STUPID

The Age of Stupid is a film released in 2009 that warns of the dangers of global warming. Its director, Franny Armstrong, decided to fund the film from a crowd of small investors who believed in her and her message. She started by finding 100 people prepared to put up £500 to cover the initial development costs.

Franny said that if the film was as successful as Michael Moore's *Fahrenheit 9/11*, investors would get around £12,500 back for their initial investment; but if it was as successful as her previous film, the sum would more likely be £12.50! In the end, more than 620 people invested £450,000 to pay for *The Age of Stupid*.

Read about how this was done, and learn how to crowdfund a film at:
www.spannerfilms.net/how_to_crowd_fund_your_film

Find out about the film at: **http://spannerfilms.net/films/ageofstupid**
Download it to show at a screening at **www.indiescreenings.net**

CROWDFUNDING WEBSITES

There are now dozens of crowdfunding websites which offer the opportunity to "invest your money" in doing good.

Buzzbnk supports social ventures which seek to change the world. For example, you can help create orchards in London, develop a new mechanism for distributing medicines in Africa using the space between the necks of cola bottles to get them to where they are needed, help build secondary schools in Uganda, produce fairtrade underwear (you get your dividend in pants) or spread the idea of TimeBanking, **www.buzzbnk.org**

Supporting social and creative projects:
Kickstarter: **www.kickstarter.com**
RocketHub: **www.rockethub.com**
IndieGoGo: **www.indiegogo.com**
33 Needs: **www.33needs.com**

Supporting music:
SellaBand: **www.sellaband.com**
SliceThePie: **www.slicethepie.com**

Supporting enterprise:
BidNetwork: **www.bidnetwork.org**
Profounder: **www.profounder.com**

Miscellaneous initiatives:
MyFootballClub, running Ebbsfleet United:
www.myfootballclub.co.uk
SpotUs, funding investigative journalism in the USA: **www.spot.us**
WellOutOfIt, a spoof website crowdfunding topical things with a social or political twist:
www.welloutofit.com

A blog about crowdfunding:
http://crowdsourcecapital.blogspot.com

The internet does not magic up the money by itself. The venturer has to create a crowd using existing contacts and networks, encouraging supporters to go out and find more supporters, and getting publicity – although some ventures will "sell themselves", such as the idea on *Kickstarter* to create a vuvuzela band to play for a day outside BP's London head-quarters to highlight the pollution from the Gulf of Mexico oil spill.

INVEST SOME MONEY IN A VENTURE TODAY

Think of a venture that you would like to raise money for, and get it going with crowdfund-ing. Use your imagination to devise something exciting. But not like *MyFreeImplants*, which crowdfunded a woman's breast implants – where the return to the "investor" is best left to the imagination: **http://myfreeimplants.com**

Click2Change URLs
www.spannerfilms.net/how_to_crowd_fund_your_film
http://spannerfilms.net/films/ageofstupid
www.indiescreenings.net
www.buzzbnk.org
www.kickstarter.com
www.rockethub.com
www.indiegogo.com
www.33needs.com
www.sellaband.com
www.slicethepie.com
www.bidnetwork.org
www.profounder.com
www.myfootballclub.co.uk
www.spot.us
www.welloutofit.com
http://crowdsourcecapital.blogspot.com
http://myfreeimplants.com

23. GET SKILLED UP FOR ACTIVISM

The 1999 demonstration in Seattle anti the *World Trade Organisation* first awoke the world to the power of internet activism. Ideas and information had sped around the world, plans had been developed and shared, people in huge numbers had arrived for a common purpose – to fight for fairer trading arrangements for the developing world. The 2008 Obama Presidential Election Campaign, the 2010 democracy movement in Egypt and across the Arab world and the 2011 Occupy movement were all made possible through social networking on *Facebook* and *Twitter*. The internet is an amazing platform for spreading ideas, and for aggregating people around issues, and for catalysing action.

If you want to become an online activist, start by learning how to do it. Download and read these training manuals:

✳ NetAction: **www.netaction.org/training**

✳ Backspace.com: **www.backspace.com/action/all.php**

✳ Amnesty's "Tools and Tips": **www.amnesty.org/en/library/info/ACT70/003/2009/en**

For a list of useful resources, go to *Planet Friendly*: **www.planetfriendly.net/active.html**

Watch the film *"Just Do It"* to see activism in action: **http://justdoitfilm.com**

GET STARTED

What issue are you going to take action on? Do you feel that with your ideas and your energy you can make a real difference? Is it something that others will want to support? Make two decisions right now: first, that you will become an online activist; second, what will be the focus of your campaign and what you would like to achieve. Your involvement needs to be distinctive – otherwise just join someone else's campaign. The next step is to gather as much information as you can about the issue and what others are doing.

GET PEOPLE

You need to find people and organisations who might be interested in your campaign. Here are some tips for doing this:

✳ *Collect e-mail addresses* from friends, colleagues and contacts at work, your *Twitter* and *Facebook* followers, parents, helpers, website visitors and anyone else you can think of. Tell everyone what you are doing.

✳ *Produce a regular e-newsletter and a blog* to tell people what's happening, and get their feedback and ideas. Ask people to pass this on.

✳ *Create a Facebook group and a Twitter account* for your campaign, and advertise this on your website and in your emails. Spend time posting information, ideas and calls to action.

✳ *Set up a website* specially for your campaign, with an easy-to-remember URL. Provide information and latest news about your campaign. Update it regularly.

✳ *Attend conferences*, and take along hand-outs, such as postcards or leaflets.

✱   *Get as much publicity as you can.* When an issue arises, you and your campaign should be already recognised as an authority on the matter.

And then…

GET ORGANISED

✱   *Invite everyone to take action,* and make it easy for them to do so. Provide them with fact sheets and other information, and suggest what they might do. Ask them to let you know what they have done and what the result was.

✱   *Move people up the "ladder of commitment".* Not everyone will do something just because you ask. If you send an email to 1,000 people, perhaps only 300 will open it, and then only 100 will take any online action (which may require little more than clicking or pasting text into an email), perhaps 30 might take offline action, and 10 might donate money to your campaign.

✱   *Nurture your core of committed supporters.* When people have done something, the next step is to thank them, and tell them the impact of their actions and what others have been doing, Then ask them do more. Over time, you will find that more people become more committed and are prepared to do more and give more for your campaign.

GET INSPIRED

Get a copy of *"Rules for Radicals"* by Saul Alinsky. This book inspired a generation of activists:
http://en.wikipedia.org/wiki/Rules_for_Radicals

Read the *Wayseer Manifesto* for a different take on what it takes to be an effective change-maker. Are you visionary, pioneering, rebellious, and irrepressible? Take a 30-second test to find out. Join the movement, read the book, watch the video: **www.wayseermanifesto.com**

GET RESULTS

Join an international campaign to end world poverty and hunger – and get *RESULTS*. RESULTS was started in the 1980s by Sam Daley-Harris, a US teacher, to try to create the political will to end hunger in a world which had all the resources to do this. Today there are *RESULTS* groups in 7 countries, where people meet together to plan campaigns. In the UK, there is an *Activist Toolkit*, and each month you get a briefing paper on a particular issue, such as the *Live Below the Line* campaign against world poverty, plus a simple action that you can download from your computer. Take action at: **www.results.org** and **www.results-uk.org**

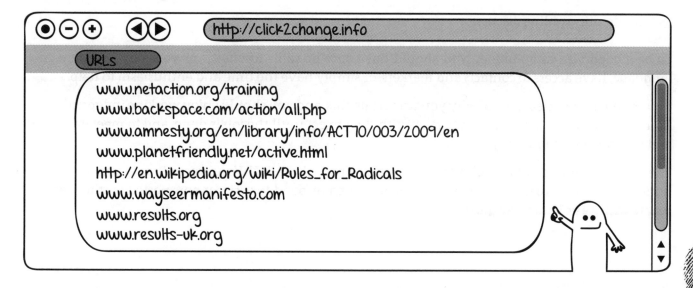

24. BECOME A VIRTUAL VOLUNTEER

Virtual Volunteering (sometimes called *Online Volunteering*) means giving some of your time to help an organisation remotely, using just your computer and the internet to connect you… plus of course your skills, your ideas and your energy. You can give practical help to projects all over the world without having to leave your home. It's really simple to do.

BECOME AN ONLINE VOLUNTEER

Whatever your skills, you can make a contribution. These are some of the skills that virtual volunteers provide:

* Language: helping translate documents

* Strategic and business planning

* Project management and evaluation

* Proposal writing

* Media: writing press releases, helping get publicity, developing campaigns

* Lobbying politicians and mobilising contacts

* Building a support network in your country

* Research: exploring specific topics and gathering data

* Design: for websites, brochures, newsletters and logos

* Photography: editing and archiving photographs

* Preparing PowerPoint presentations

* Computing: designing databases and simple accounting systems

* Professional expertise (such as advising on business, legal and marketing matters, developing training courses or providing organic farming know how)

* Mentoring the project leader

* Moderating online discussions

To be a good virtual volunteer, you should have specific skills to offer… or you may be fluent in a language, have access to contacts and markets, or simply have the time and enthusiasm to help.

You should have a clear idea of why you want to do this, and you should enjoy working independently. You need to make a commitment to stick with the project until the job is done, and to meet deadlines and answer emails promptly

The United Nations online volunteering website (part of the *UN Volunteers Programme*) acts as a notice board for virtual volunteers. Register, and then respond to assignments posted on the website. **www.onlinevolunteering.org**

MICRO-VOLUNTEER

Here's a way of working with others on a particular task or to solve a problem, contributing as much or as little as you feel able. Just sign up with *Sparked*, indicating your interests and skills. You will be offered appropriate challenges which need to be completed within a specific timescale. For example, if you are interested in human rights and want to help with copywriting, a human rights organisation might be asking people to critique its website or help it find a name for a new magazine. Do this at **www.sparked.com**

BE A GOOD NABUUR

NABUUR.com is a Dutch foundation which provides communities in developing countries (called "Villages") access to resources to solve their problems via a network of virtual volunteers (called "Neighbours").

This is how it works:

1. A community needs help. After an initial assessment, the Village is given a page on *NABUUR.com*.

2. A representative of the local community then describes a problem or task that needs to be undertaken.

3. People wanting to volunteer sign up on the website. They select a Village to help (these are listed by country and by type of activity). Or you can browse the tasks that need undertaking until you find something of interest.

4. Along with other Neighbours, you try to solve the problem. The best solutions are proposed to the Village.

5. The Village decides what to do; the solutions are implemented.

6. The Neighbours are kept in touch through photos and stories posted on the *NABUUR.com* website.

Over 37,500 Neighbours from all over the world are assisting 293 Villages in 31 countries. They may be searching for information on low-cost latrines or high-yielding crops, finding a market for local crafts, fixing up a school to twin with, helping set up a community radio station, arranging the donation of computers. Here are two examples:

Mumias, Kenya: In Luhya village in western Kenya, most houses are mud-walled with thatched roofs. Villagers want basic education and health care. But first they want to encourage income generation and create employment. They need ideas for micro-enterprises and projects that could be replicated in Mumias.

Chimaltenango, Guatemala: The Kaqchikel Maya are peasant farmers, growing maize, beans and vegetables. The population has grown rapidly in recent years, which has led to widespread deforestation. To develop alternative sources of income, Villagers want to develop ecotourism. The local area has beautiful forests (despite deforestation), volcanoes, ancient temples and indigenous arts and crafts. The community needs to know what sorts of activities could be organised for tourists and how to promote the Village as an eco-tourist destination.

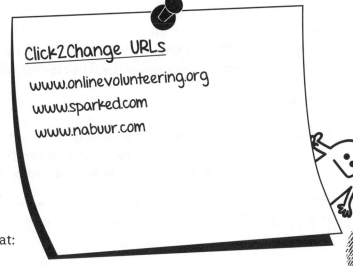

Click2Change URLs

www.onlinevolunteering.org
www.sparked.com
www.nabuur.com

Help a Village, which is often isolated and in a poor country and which may need your skills. *Join a thematic group* with issues ranging from sustainable agriculture to story-telling.

Become a good Neighbour. Sign up now at: **www.nabuur.com**

25. DISTRIBUTE FREE SOFTWARE

The *Free/Libre and Open Source Software* movement (often called *FLOSS*) is built on the ideals of collaboration and sharing. This is in refreshing contrast to the world of private property and profit that we have become used to.

When programmers can read, redistribute, and modify the source code for a piece of software, the software evolves. People all over the world improve it, fix the bugs, adapt it for new purposes. And this happens at a speed that seems astonishing, in comparison with the much slower pace of conventional software development. You only have to contrast the evolution of the *MS Windows* operating system (owned by *Microsoft*) with *Linux* (free); or *Encyclopaedia Britannica* (proprietary) with *Wikipedia* (open source).

Free Software means software freedom. It provides these four freedoms:

＊ To run the programme for any purpose *(Freedom 0)*.

＊ To study how the programme works and adapt it *(Freedom 1)*.

＊ To redistribute copies *(Freedom 2)*.

＊ To improve the programme and release the improvements to others *(Freedom 3)*.

Open Source Software is not the same as Free Software. Open Source provides software developers with free access to the source code. This generates better quality, more reliable, more flexible and lower-cost software solutions. Open Source is required for Software Freedoms 1 and 3.

The internet is fuelling the growth of open source systems, and not just for software development. Read *"Wikinomics"* by Don Tapscott and Anthony Williams to understand how *"mass collaboration is changing everything"*.

Software Freedom Day each September promotes the idea of *Free and Open Source Software*. Find out about the day and how you can participate: **www.softwarefreedomday.org**

Free Software Foundation develops Free Software. It has created the GNU *"Copyleft"* licensing system for making Free Software available whilst protecting copyright, and it publishes an online Directory of Free Software. **www.gnu.org**

Open Source Initiative promotes Open Source development of software. **www.opensource.org**

Here's a story from Macedonia: *"Our organisation, Free/Libre Software Macedonia, bought and recorded 1,000 CD's with free software (OpenCD/Knoppix) which we gave out to coincide with the opening of the Microsoft office in Skopje. We called the operation "Free Software Flood" because it was raining like hell that day and because all the participants where "flooded" with free open software."*

USE LINUX

Linux is a PC operating system originally created by Linus Torvalds with the assistance of developers around the world. *Linux* is freely available to everyone. Some countries, including Brazil, are adopting Linux as their country standard. **www.linux.com** and **http://en.wikipedia.org/wiki/Linux**

"Ubuntu" is a Xhosa word which embodies the concept of mutual well-being – *"I'm OK if you're OK"*. The *Ubuntu Manifesto* states that software should be available free of charge, software tools should be

usable by people in their local language, and people should have the freedom to customise and alter their software however they see fit. Download *Ubuntu Linux* at: **www.ubuntu.com**

Ubuntu is funded by Mark Shuttleworth, a young South African entrepreneur who achieved fame as a space tourist, paying around $20 million to travel on a Russian Soyuz TM-34.

✳ Find out more about Mark at **www.africaninspace.com**

✳ Localising free software is a key element of bridging the digital divide, Help translate free software into one of the 11 official South African languages: **www.translate.org.za**

MAKE A MOVE TO OPENOFFICE

MS Office has become the standard software package for office use. But there is a free and some say better alternative called *OpenOffice.org*.

1. Download OOo from **www.openoffice.org**

2. Use it yourself. Take pride in striking a blow for software freedom.

3. Tell others, pass on the download URL.

DISTRIBUTE FREE SOFTWARE TO SCHOOLS

Richard Stallman, the founding father of the *FLOSS* movement, argues that schools should exclusively use free software because:

1. It saves money; even in the rich world, schools are short of funds.

2. It teaches students the ideas of cooperation.

Free Software could be promoted just like recycling. In France and Italy, groups are planning a *Libre Software School Day*.

There is a lot of free software that is suitable for use in schools. Including the following:

✳ **Chemtool**, for drawing organic molecules.

✳ **ECell System**, for modelling, simulation, and analysis of biological cells.

✳ **GenChemLab,** for helping students prepare for actual lab experience through experiments in titration, calorimetry, vapour pressure, electrochemistry.

✳ **Earth3D**, for visualising the earth in real time in 3D. You can rotate and zoom the view until countries, cities and even single houses become visible.

✳ **Calcoo**, for scientific calculations.

✳ **Dr Genius**, for vector drawing.

For a fuller list go to **http://wikiwikiweb.de/FlossInSchools**

Research what's available, and then go and tell your local secondary school armed with a short manifesto on using FLOSS.

www.softwarefreedomday.org
www.gnu.org
www.opensource.org
www.linux.com
http://en.wikipedia.org/wiki/Linux
www.ubuntu.com
www.africaninspace.com
www.translate.org.za
www.openoffice.org
http://wikiwikiweb.de/FlossInSchools

26. BECOME AN ONLINE EDITOR

The process of organising all the world's knowledge in a single place was started by the Greeks. Making all knowledge available to everyone became the aim of the *Encyclopaedists* during the 18th century French Enlightenment. These attempts continued into the 20th century, with the world's knowledge growing exponentially, through publications such as *Encyclopaedia Britannica* and *Chambers*.

If you had the task of collecting together all of the world's knowledge, would you hire a team of editors and pay expert contributors to write articles on each topic? This would involve a huge amount of organisation and up-front investment, and inevitably reflect a social or political bias (too much emphasis on the European perspective, not enough sensitivity to gender, etc.). Because of all the work involved, it would be expensive to buy and to keep up to date, even as an e-Book.

Now thanks to the internet and a technique called *Wiki* (which means *"quick"* in Hawaiian), there is an alternative.

WIKIPEDIA

Wikipedia was started in 2001 as an "open encyclopaedia". In its first year over 20,000 entries were created. By September 2004, the millionth article was completed. By 2011, there were more than 91,000 active contributors and 17 million articles in more than 270 languages, 3.62 million of which are in English.

Articles can be created or edited by anyone (except by banned users and there are a few protected pages). Contributions have to comply with *Wikipedia's Neutral Point of View* policy, so that there is no bias in what is published. The entries in the encyclopaedia develop as amendments and additions are made. Flaws are quickly repaired. Every day sees tens of thousands of edits and thousands of new articles. Everything is copyright free.

You can play a part in the world's largest information project by doing these things:

1. Use *Wikipedia* as your starting point for finding out about something. You will seldom be disappointed! **http://en.wikipedia.org**

2. Take the *Wikipedia* tutorial on writing and editing: **http://en.wikipedia.org/wiki/Wikipedia:Tutorial**

3. Write an article for *Wikipedia*. Start by finding out whether the subject already has an entry. You might think about writing an article on your community, the hobby you are passionate about, a topic you're expert on.

4. Or, take a subject you know about, find the *Wikipedia* entry… and edit it, adding missing bits.

Wikipedia is a project of the *Wikimedia Foundation*: **www.wikimediafoundation.org**

Other Wikimedia projects include:
Wikibooks, copyright-free textbooks and manuals: **www.wikibooks.org**
Wikiversity, free learning tools: **www.wikiversity.org**
Wiktionary, a Wiki dictionary: **www.wiktionary.org**
Wikiquote, copyright-free quotations: **www.wikiquote.org**
Wikisource, copyright-free documents: **http://wikisource.org**
Wikispecies, an encyclopaedia of species: **http://species.wikimedia.org/wiki/Wikispecies**

TWO OTHER WIKI PROJECTS

wikiHow is building the world's largest how-to manual, which aims to offer solutions to every problem that anybody might encounter in their lives. It currently contains over 105,000 articles. These are just some of the topics covered:

How to help a cat give birth

How to make toffee apples

How to serve a bagel breakfast

How to save your home from foreclosure

How to quit Facebook

How to care for a toad

www.wikihow.com

Wikitravel aims to create a free, complete, up-to-date and reliable worldwide travel guide. There are 25,000 destination guides and other articles written and edited by wiki-travellers from around the globe. If you are travelling anywhere, this (along with *TripAdvisor:* **www.tripadvisor.co.uk**) is a place to find out more. If you've just got back, edit an entry with your experiences and suggestions. **http://wikitravel.org**

OTHER OPPORTUNITIES FOR BECOMING AN ONLINE EDITOR

Editors wanted: *Project Gutenberg* is creating an online library of copyright-free books. A book is first machine-converted into an electronic copy. This is then proof-read twice by volunteer *"Distributed Proofreaders"* all over the world. There are now over 100,000 books available from *Project Gutenberg* and its partners. **www.gutenberg.org**

Translators wanted: In France in 1751-1772, the *"Enclyclopedie"* attempted to put all human knowledge between two covers. It comprised 28 volumes, 71,818 articles and 2,885 illustrations. A second expanded edition in 66 volumes was published in 1782-1832. Help the *University of Michigan* translate the *"Enclyclopedie"* into English: **http://quod.lib.umich.edu/d/did/index.html**

Cataloguers wanted: The *Open Directory Project* aims to become the definitive catalogue of websites and pages. Sign up as a cataloguer. First choose a topic you know something about and help make the web more accessible. **www.dmoz.org**

Share what you've created – photos, videos, a theory or an equation, slogans, recipes, poems, music. Help create a "world bank" of common property for the benefit of all, instead of tying your work up in copyright restrictions. Deposit the best of what you've created at *Creative Commons*. **http://creativecommons.org**

Click2Change URLs

http://en.wikipedia.org

http://en.wikipedia.org/wiki/Wikipedia:Tutorial

www.wikimediafoundation.org

www.wikibooks.org

www.wikiversity.org

www.wiktionary.org

www.wikiquote.org

http://wikisource.org

http://species.wikimedia.org/wiki/Wikispecies

www.wikihow.com

www.tripadvisor.co.uk

http://wikitravel.org

www.gutenberg.org

http://quod.lib.umich.edu/d/did/index.html

www.dmoz.org

http://creativecommons.org

27. BECOME AN ONLINE MENTOR

A mentor is someone who acts as a trusted friend to a person in need of help or support, and who gives advice when asked.

Mentors are ordinary people who are prepared to spend around a couple of hours a week for at least a year, connecting up, listening to what their mentee (the person being mentored) has to say, responding to their questions and problems... possibly undertaking everyday activities, such as playing football or computer games, going shopping or just having a coffee together.

Mentees are often young people at risk, where their mentor can give them a life-changing experience. Mentees can also be mentors, receiving advice and support when they need it, but also giving it to others when they ask.

Mentoring is a great way to volunteer. It is usually carried out in person face-to-face; but it can also be done online or by telephone or by video *Skype*. You don't need any formal training. So why not sign up as an online mentor? Give a little bit of your time to help someone who needs a bit of help.

DO IT THROUGH THE HORSE'S MOUTH

Horsesmouth is a specialist e-mentoring website. Mentors provide:

* **Life advice** on relationships and family, health and wellbeing, passions and talents, beliefs and identity, rights and law, home and money, citizenship and volunteering.

* **Work advice** on choosing or changing career, getting a job, managing a business, rights at work, working relationships, workplace bullying, stress and work-life balance, retirement.

* **Learning advice** to help the mentee figure out issues around education, skills and training.

At *Horsesmouth*, you don't meet your mentee, so you are less likely to be judgmental or to tell them what you think they want to hear. *"Think of it as providing the kindness of a stranger... on tap!"*

Horsesmouth has developed some "cool tools" for its mentors:

* *The M-Factor*, a points scheme that helps measure the success of mentoring.

* *Pearls of Wisdom*, a space where mentors can share thoughts about specific topics – anything from an anecdote to a slice of personal philosophy.

* *Your Library*, where you share your favourite books and websites with other mentors and mentees.

* *Tags*, which are keywords attached to profiles, which you add to your profile to help others find you.

* *Manage your time*, to track the time you spend on the site.

To become a mentor, you first sign up, then submit your mentor profile for approval and get registered. Those requiring mentoring then view your profile and contact you, asking you to become their mentor. **www.horsesmouth.co.uk**

WHAT CAN MENTORING DO?

Adam attends *Alcoholics Anonymous*, Bilal runs a business, Chris studies chemistry at college and Diane lives with diabetes. What do they all have in common? They could all share the lessons they've learned from experience with people facing similar situations.

What's in it for the mentor? Drawing on your life experiences to help others can be rewarding. It is an easy and enjoyable way to give something back. If you're a younger person, it can build skills that employers value (such as listening, problem solving and learning from experience).

What's in it for the mentee? Communicating with someone who has experienced what you are experiencing or who understands you and your problems can be really helpful. While it may not be a substitute for proper professional advice or for the support that family and friends can give, sometimes it's exactly what the mentee needs.

BRIGHTSIDEUNIAID

This e-mentoring service is specifically targeted to help young people aged 14 to 25 from socially disadvantaged backgrounds. The mentoring aims to help them:

✳ Feel inspired and confident

✳ Explore their options

✳ Build skills, get informed and prepared

✳ Make the right choices for their future.

If you feel you can help, sign up at: **www.brightsideuniaid.org**

OPEN SOURCE MENTORING WITH INMO

The *International Mentoring Network Organisation* was launched in 2003 by three university students who wanted to connect the concepts of open source and professional mentoring. Their idea was to enable people to interview their ideal mentor and then to share the mentor's advice, knowledge, and vision with the rest of the world by putting it on the website.

Browse this website, and pick up pearls of wisdom from some of the mentors that have been interviewed. Join the Network, and ask questions of mentors through scheduled interviews.

Sign up to be a mentor if you are a successful professional and feel that you have experience and ideas that you can share with others. **www.imno.org**

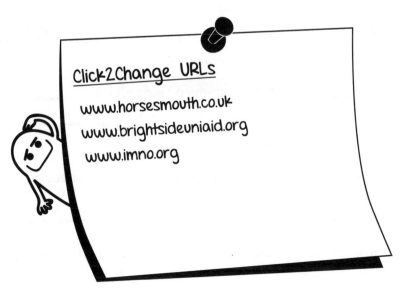

Click2Change URLS

www.horsesmouth.co.uk

www.brightsideuniaid.org

www.imno.org

28. TRY VIRAL MARKETING

Your task is to spread a message around the world.

Your uncle has been arrested in Turkey for standing up for human rights. There are rumours he is being tortured. You want to get as many people as possible to write to the Turkish Prime Minister protesting the situation and appealing for his speedy release. You contact your 100 friends on *FaceBook* and *Twitter* followers requesting that they write a letter. You also ask them to open up their address book and send the same letter to their own friends. And if these people then write to a hundred of their friends, and if each of these writes to a hundred of their friends, then you will have reached out to 1 million people.

But it never works out quite like this. Firstly, most people don't respond – either through inertia or because they do not share your point of view. Secondly, many of their friends will be your friends. And thirdly, when your friends ask their friends, the impact is that much less because the connection is at one remove.

But if sufficient people read the letter and act and pass it on, it will spread rather like a virus – which is why this technique is called "Viral Marketing".

Viral marketing is nothing new. Chain letters asking people to send £5 promising them a larger sum from people further down the chain is viral marketing prompted by greed. But the internet makes the technique much more powerful, because it's quick and it's free.

DEVELOP A VIRAL CAMPAIGN

Whether it is the poisoning of a community through open-cast mining in Chile, or a human rights issue in Turkey, or urging the world community to do something in Darfur, or a campaign urging Bill Gates to do something once and for all about internet spam, or just litter and graffiti polluting the streets of your city, devise a message which will spread. Send it out and see what happens. Google *"Viral Marketing"* for inspiration. Now try to *"End Hate"* virally:

> What if we all decided, starting right now ... that the color of our skins' didn't matter?
>
>  or religion?
>
> or nationality?
>
> or ideology?
>
> What if we stopped being afraid?
>
> Think about it for a minute ... maybe it wouldn't be that hard to live in peace?
>
> Maybe it's just that simple.
>
> It's estimated that there are 605,000,000 people on earth with internet access. If 100,000,000 see this message can they make a difference? Forward this.

Spread this message to end hate in the world (based on a campaign run by *EndHate* in 2007).

SIX DEGREES OF SEPARATION

The theory of six degrees of separation states that any person is linked to any other person on Earth by just six ties. This can't be absolutely proved, but seems to be true: **http://en.wikipedia.org/wiki/Six_degrees_of_separation**

Actor Kevin Bacon claimed that he had worked with everyone in Hollywood – now you can test his claim. Play the game *"Six Degrees of Kevin Bacon"* to determine the degree of separation between any two actors alive or dead: **www.thekevinbacongame.com** And join Kevin's campaign to spread a ripple of good across the USA: **www.sixdegrees.org**

FREE HUGS

Juan Mann started the Free Hugs campaign in 2004.

"I'd been living in London when my world turned upside down and I had to come home. By the time my plane landed back in Sydney, all I had left was a carry on bag full of clothes and a world of troubles.

I wanted someone out there to be waiting for me… to be happy to see me… to smile at me… to hug me. So I got some cardboard and a marker and made a sign. I found the busiest pedestrian intersection in the city and held that sign aloft, with the words "Free Hugs" on both sides.

For 15 minutes, people just stared right through me. The first person who stopped, tapped me on the shoulder and told me how her dog had just died that morning… how that morning had been the one-year anniversary of her only daughter dying in a car accident… how what she needed now was a hug.

I got down on one knee, we put our arms around each other and when we parted, she was smiling."

The *Free Hugs* movement really took off when Juan Mann posted his *Free Hugs* video on *YouTube* on 22nd September 2006. It was viewed over 10 million times in the following 3 months. *Free Hugs* groups have sprung up all over the world.

Free Hugs: **www.freehugscampaign.org**
Search *Juan Mann's Free Hugs* videos: **www.dailymotion.com**

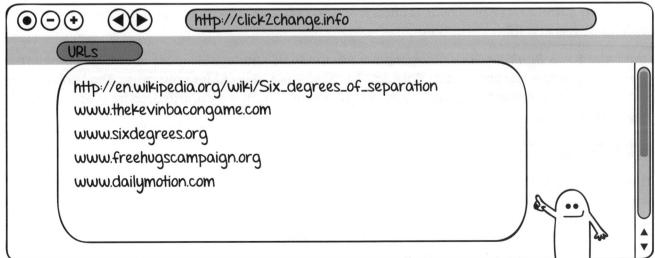

http://click2change.info

URLs

http://en.wikipedia.org/wiki/Six_degrees_of_separation
www.thekevinbacongame.com
www.sixdegrees.org
www.freehugscampaign.org
www.dailymotion.com

29. PUBLISH IT YOURSELF

You can publish your very own book for well under $10!

Using the technology of print-on-demand, where printing presses are set up to print individual copies, combined with an internet-based system for uploading your typescript and turning it into a final design, *Lulu.com* and *Blurb.com* have created a really cheap and simple way of getting a book published.

Whether you want to produce just a single copy to take to an interview to impress your interviewers or to show the audience at a conference you are speaking at, or 25 copies to give to your friends next Christmas, or 500 copies to sell at book readings, or an e-book to send around the world, *Lulu* and *Blurb* provide you with an easy way of becoming a published author.

There are no up-front printing bills. There are no storage problems – you don't have to order, pay for and warehouse large numbers of copies of your book. You just get copies printed as you need them. And unlike being published commercially, you, the author, retain complete control over content and design.

Go to *Lulu* or *Blurb*; start uploading your text and illustrations into your chosen format using the tools provided for doing this.

LULU

"Ever hear the phrase 'Boy, that's a real lulu'?. Well, even if you haven't, think of the word 'Lulu' as an old-fashioned term for a remarkable person, object or idea. Quite frankly, that's exactly what Lulu, the company, is. Think of us as an open marketplace for digital content. An on-demand publishing tool for books, e-books, music, images, movies and calendars." – Lulu describing itself

You can publish and sell books, pamphlets, music, comics, photographs and movies on *Lulu*. The website provides simple instructions for turning your manuscript into a book. *Lulu* manages the printing, delivery and customer service. You can take delivery of the books and sell them yourself. Or you can set your own royalty and use the *Lulu* website for marketing the books and getting orders for copies. *Lulu* takes a percentage from each transaction to cover its costs. **www.lulu.com**

BLURB

Blurb offers a similar service to *Lulu*. It offers five sizes of colour book and two for black and white text, with hardcover and softcover options.

Blurb also has a *Blurb for Good* programme for individuals and organisations wanting to promote a cause. You produce the book, set its price and keep 100% of the profit for your cause. The book will be featured in the *Blurb Bookstore* and you might qualify for a charitable contribution for every book sold. **www.blurb.com**

HOW MUCH WILL IT COST?

These are some sample costings from *Blurb* to give you a rough idea of how much publishing a book will cost (shipping is extra, with discounts for more than 10 copies):

      6 x 9 inches, black and white text, 160 pages, colour cover
          paperback, $6.95 per copy; hardback $23.95 per copy
      7 x 7 inches, full colour, 120 pages
          paperback, $21.95 per copy, hardback, $35.95 per copy

BECOME A PUBLISHED AUTHOR TODAY!

Do one of these things right now:

✴ *Get your manuscript out of the drawer* where it has been gathering dust for years – or rather, find it on your computer's hard drive. Give it an editorial once-over to make sure it makes sense and to remove all the typos (remember that *rubbish in = rubbish out*)…

✴ *Or write your soon-to-become-a-best-seller* today on a subject that you feel passionate about…

✴ *Or create an instant book* by doing some quick research on the internet on a subject that you are interested in, such as: *"50 things you can do right now to stop global warming"* or *"How to give yourself away: recycling your body and everything you own"*.

✴ *Or create a notebook* with just blank pages but with a bright cover and a snappy title which shows you as an expert when you wave it around, with a title such as: *"How to become a guru"* or *"How to end world poverty"*.

Upload your manuscript and a design for the cover on to *Lulu* or *Blurb*, and follow the instructions.

WHAT'S THE ODDEST BOOK TITLE?

Vote for your favourite book title on the shortlist announced in March each year for The *Bookseller/ Diagram Prize for Oddest Title of the Year*. The 2010 shortlist included:

>   Afterthoughts of a Worm Hunter
>   Crocheting Adventures with Hyperbolic Planes
>   Governing Lethal Behavior in Autonomous Robots

Previous years titles have included:

>   Better Never To Have Been: The Harm of Coming Into Existence
>   How Green Were the Nazis?

http://en.wikipedia.org/wiki/Bookseller/Diagram_Prize_for_Oddest_Title_of_the_Year
www.thebookseller.com/diagram-prize

New Message ⊖ ▣ ⊗

File   Edit   View   Insert   Format   Tools   Message   Help

✉➤
Send

From: click2change@gmail.com

To:

Cc:

Subject: URLs

www.lulu.com
www.blurb.com
http://en.wikipedia.org/wiki/Bookseller/Diagram_Prize_for_Oddest_Title_of_the_Year
www.thebookseller.com/diagram-prize

30. DESIGN YOUR OWN T-SHIRT

You can design your own t-shirt, get it made and then sell it… and perhaps even make a profit. You can do all this on the internet – without even having to get up from the chair you are sitting on and with surprisingly little financial outlay.

Pick a cause; write a slogan; put it on a t-shirt. Then order your t-shirts printed with this slogan… and wear them or give them away or sell them to spread the word. Organise a stunt or a photocall to take the message even further. Check out the following websites:

www.streetshirts.co.uk   www.spreadshirt.co.uk   www.zazzle.co.uk

There are lots of other suppliers. Just type *"Make your own t-shirt"* into *Google* and take your pick from what comes up. Here are a few ideas for the sorts of message to put on your t-shirt.

PUT HUMAN RIGHTS ON A T-SHIRT

Design and print a range of t-shirts each featuring a basic human right. Choose from this list which sets out all our rights as set out in the Articles of the UN's *Universal Declaration of Human Rights* (which most countries have signed up to):

1. All human beings are born free and equal
2. Human rights are for everyone
3. We have a right to life, liberty and security of person
4. Slavery and the slave trade are banned
5. No one shall be tortured
6. We all have a right to an identity
7. All are equal before the law
8. There must be effective remedy for human rights violations
9. No arbitrary arrest, detention or exile
10. We have a right to a fair trial
11. We should be presumed innocent until proved guilty
12. No arbitrary interference with privacy, family, home or correspondence
13. We have a right to freedom of movement
14. We have a right to asylum from persecution
15. We have a right to a nationality
16. We have a right to marry and found a family
17. We have a right to own property
18. We have a right to freedom of thought, conscience and religion
19. We have a right to freedom of opinion and expression
20. We have a right to freedom of peaceful assembly and association
21. We have a right to take part in the government of your country
22. We have a right to social security
23. We have a right to work and to equal pay
24. We have a right to rest and leisure
25. We have a right to an adequate standard of living
26. We have a right to education
27. We have a right to participate in cultural life
28. Rights and freedoms should be fully realised internationally
29. Everyone has duties to the community
30. No right to destroy basic human rights

Find out more about the Universal Declaration of Human Rights at:
http://en.wikipedia.org/wiki/Universal_Declaration_of_Human_Rights
http://www.un.org/rights

TAKE ACTION ON AN INTERNATIONAL DAY

The UN designates international years. 2011 focussed on chemistry, forests, youth and people of African descent: **www.un.org/observances/years.shtml** There are also designated days for everything from AIDS to water, poetry and mother languages. Choose an upcoming international day and produce a t-shirt with a slogan for it:

Official days:
http://portal.unesco.org/en/ev.php-URL_ID=7588&URL_DO=DO_TOPIC&URL_SECTION=201.html

Unofficial days: (which might be more fun):
http://homeschooling.about.com/od/fundaycalendars/index_a.htm

Plant a tree: A voice from the past… these are three slogans from the *International Tree Planting Year* 1973:

Plant a tree in '73   Plant one more in '74   Will it thrive in '75?

We obviously did not do well enough, because in 2006, the United Nations launched its Billion Trees campaign, and by 2011 pledges had been received to plant over 13 billion trees; and there's even a petition seeking a million signatories to plant a Trillion Trees: **www.unep.org/billiontreecampaign**

A HEMP T-SHIRT MIGHT BE THE ANSWER

Cotton growing has an environmental impact. It is creating serious water problems in countries such as Egypt and Pakistan. The cotton needed to make just one t-shirt requires 1,170 litres of water – that's more than a tonne; and the intensively irrigated fields then become salty, which turns productive land into desert.

So next time you buy a t-shirt with a message on fair trade, just remember to balance the good of helping tea workers earn a fair wage with the impact that producing that t-shirt has had on the local environment.

Why not switch to hemp? Hemp is from the cannabis plant – *Cannabis Sativa* – but used for non-drug purposes. It is a coarse linen-like fibre which is mostly used for sacks and floor coverings because of its strength and durability. Garments made of hemp have a rougher finish if they are made from 100% hemp. For t-shirts, the usual mix is 55% hemp, 45% cotton.

Buy hemp t-shirts from from *The Hemp Store* in sand, black, navy, natural, olive and dark red, £17.50:
www.thehempstore.co.uk

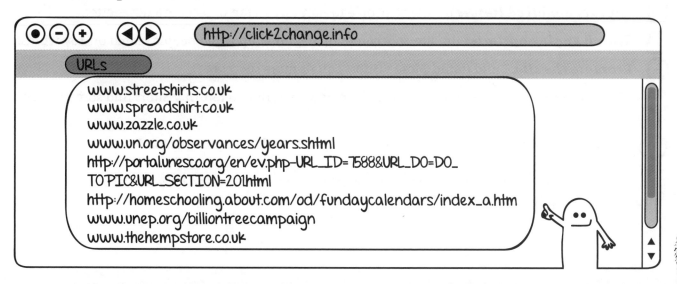

31. BUILD YOUR OWN WEBSITE

French philosopher Rene Descartes declared *"Cogito ergo sum"* – which is Latin for *"I think, therefore I am"*. He was looking for certainties in life. One thing he was absolutely certain about was that he was thinking. And this led him to another certainty – that in order to think, he must exist.

In today's "Wonderful World of the World Wide Web", you might extend this idea to *"I have a website, therefore I exist"*. If someone wants to find out more about you, your ideas, your organisation and the causes you are involved with, then the first thing they will do is type your name into *Google*. If the search comes up with nothing, then as far as the searcher is concerned you just don't exist! So it's really important to have a web presence.

CREATING A WEBSITE

Your website could be for:

✳ You, yourself.

✳ Your family, now and in the past. You can also pin your family at Historypin: **www.historypin.com**

✳ Any special interest you have… such as campaigning to save endangered species.

✳ The organisation that you have started in order to turn your ideas into action.

✳ Your local community.

Here are ten key steps to creating a website:

1. *Plan the site.* Think clearly about why you want it and what you want your visitors to do.

2. *Choose a domain name.* Make this simple, and something that clearly reflects what your website is about. Find what's available at **www.1and1.co.uk** and **www.godaddy.com**

3. *Find a hosting company* for your website.

4. *Design and build the website.* It should look good. But more importantly, the information should be clearly organised and the website should be easy to use. Google *"Design your own website"* for how-to advice.

5. Think of ways using your website to **generate or raise income**.

6. *Capture e-mail addresses* by asking people to sign up as a fan or receive a newsletter.

7. *Search engine optimise* the site, so it comes up near the top when people search on key words.

8. *Promote the site.* Build traffic. More visitors equals more success.

9. *Maintain the site.* Keep it up to date. Put up new material, so return visitors find something of interest.

10. *Monitor visitors* and where they come from. Simple tools are available for this.

That's all there is to it. Simple! But if it's too complicated or time-consuming for you, just put your effort into creating a really great *Facebook* page.

FACILITIES TO INCLUDE ON YOUR WEBSITE

There are all sorts of features you can include. Here are a few to think about:

Have a dashboard. Use *NetVibes* which provides a one-click access to lots of different facilities, such as pages on networking sites or even the weather: **www.netvibes.com**

Post still pictures at one of these: *Flickr* at **www.flickr.com** or *Tabblo* at **www.tabblo.com**

Post video material on *YouTube*: **www.youtube.com**

Have a *FaceBook* page or create a *Facebook* campaign: **www.facebook.com**

Link to your *Twitter* account: **www.twitter.com**

Recommend books at *LibraryThing*: **www.librarything.com**

Display and tag your favourite documents at *Delicious*: **http://www.delicious.com**

Create your own blog at *Blogger*: **www.blogger.com** or *WordPress*: **http://wordpress.com**

MAKING MONEY FROM YOUR WEBSITE

Here are some ways of making money from your website:

(1.) *Sell things* – goods and services. You will need a payment mechanism such as *PayPal* for the transactions.

(2.) *Sign up to Google AdSense*, and make money from advertising and 'click-throughs'.

(3.) *Join an affiliate programme*, such as *Amazon*, where you get a (small) percentage of the commerce arising from your site (such as sale of books).

(4.) *Solicit funds*. Don't just ask for money; suggest practical ways in which people can get involved. Use *JustGiving* to handle donations **www.justgiving.com**. Or **www.buzzbnk.org** to crowdfund a project.

WEB HOSTING WITH A DIFFERENCE

If you are green at heart, why not get hosted using 100% solar power! Through massive arrays of solar panels in the Californian dessert, and an eco-friendly data centre heated by the warmth of the machines and cooled by the external environment (no air-con), get your website hosted through **www.solarhost.co.uk**.

Battery banks store months of energy so services are not interrupted at night or during the winter months. In case of emergencies, there is a generator as a back-up – but this is never used. Using solar hosting allows you to proudly state that your website is eco-friendly and 100% carbon neutral.

MEET TIM BERNERS-LEE

Tim Berners-Lee devised the World Wide Web, one of the great ideas of the 20th century, which has profoundly changed all our lives. Find out about Tim at: **http://en.wikipedia.org/wiki/Tim_Berners-Lee** and **www.w3.org/People/Berners-Lee**

Click2Change URLs
www.1and1.co.uk
www.godaddy.com
www.netvibes.com
www.flickr.com
www.tabblo.com
www.youtube.com
www.facebook.com
www.twitter.com
www.librarything.com
http://www.delicious.com
www.blogger.com
http://wordpress.com
www.justgiving.com
www.buzzbnk.org
www.solarhost.co.uk
http://en.wikipedia.org/wiki/Tim_Berners-Lee
www.w3.org/People/Berners-Lee

32. ENGAGE IN THE DEMOCRATIC PROCESS

The internet is transforming the democratic process by making your elected representatives a whole lot easier to reach – this in turn makes them more accountable to you and their electorate (even if you voted for the other guy or didn't vote at all, they are there to represent everyone in their constituency *including you*).

WRITE TO YOUR ELECTED REPRESENTATIVE

WriteToThem.com is a UK website which enables you to write to your elected representative with just a click of your mouse. You can write to your Member of Parliament, Member of the European Parliament, Member of the Scottish, Welsh and London Assemblies and your local councillors.

Contact your elected representative today on a matter of burning concern to you or your local community. It's easy. You just do the following:

1. Go to the *WriteToThem* website.

2. Type in your full UK postcode. Click *"Go"*.

3. You will be given a list of all your elected representatives. Click on the person you want to write to.

4. Write your letter. Send it by clicking *"Submit"*.

5. You will receive an e-mail asking you to confirm that you wish to send the letter. Click the link. That's it!

6. Most reply within two weeks, sometimes at length and in detail, responding to your concerns and stating their position.

If you think their answer is unsatisfactory, write to them again telling them so. If you want to meet them face-to-face to pursue the matter further, telephone their office to find out when their next "surgery" is. Book an appointment or just turn up,

You can magnify the impact, by getting lots of people to write their own letters in their own words expressing the same concerns about the same issue. If everyone sends identical letters, this might be seen as junk mail. Elected representatives get surprisingly few letters, and they use their "postbag" to assess public opinion – which influences their views.

HEAR HOW WELL THEY ARE DOING

You can find out more about who your MP is, what they are interested in and how they have performed in Parliament by going to *theyworkforyou.com* and entering your postcode. **www.theyworkforyou. com**

Press your MP to give you regular news about what they're doing. Join *Your Constituency Mailing List*. Go to *hearfromyourmp.com*. Enter your details, and you'll be added to a queue of other people in your constituency who want to hear more from your MP. When enough people have signed up, the MP will be sent an e-mail which will say *"20 or 50 or 500 of your constituents want to hear about what you are up to"*. When the MP replies, you will be able to join a forum to discuss what they say. **www.hearfromyourmp.com**

All these services have been developed by *My Society*, which aims to enhance democracy using the internet: **www.mysociety.org**

Find out more about the *UK Parliament* and how it works: **www.parliament.uk**

WRITE TO A LORD

The Upper Chamber in the *UK Parliament* is a completely unelected body consisting entirely appointed hereditary and life peers (Lords) and a few judges and bishops who are there because of their job. There are Lords who are affiliated to one of the political parties as well as "cross-benchers" with no party affiliation.

Send a letter to a Lord today. Go to **www.writetothem.com/lords** to find a Lord with a known interest in your issue, or who has some association with a particular place, or who shares your birthday (that gives an opportunity for an interesting introductory line in your letter), or just write to a random Lord.

MAKE SURE YOU VOTE

The proportion of people voting in UK elections has been declining. This is not good for democracy. It is important that you vote, even if you want to spoil your vote by writing *"Elections are useless"* on the ballot paper. In Australia, voting is compulsory – which is one way of ensuring a high turnout!.

Make sure that you register and get on the Electoral Roll. Then vote for the best candidate or the candidate who best reflects your views. If you are well-organised, try to arrange to vote in a marginal constituency, where your vote really can make a difference.

GET ELECTED....

....this could be your first step towards running the country. If you are ambitious, put yourself forward as a candidate in a parliamentary General Election or By-Election. If you want to follow a more traditional route, become a local councillor first.

Find out who is eligible to stand and what to do: **www.electoralcommission.org.uk**

Click2Change URLs:

www.theyworkforyou.com

www.hearfromyourmp.com

www.mysociety.org

www.parliament.uk

www.writetothem.com/lords

www.electoralcommission.org.uk

33. BECOME AN ONLINE GURU

If you have something to say, the internet provides you with an unparalleled opportunity for getting your message out – although you also have to find people prepared to listen to you. And if you end up knowing more about a particular issue than anyone else, you could even end up as an online guru!

BECOME A BLOGGER

A BLOG (weB-LOG) is a place where you can post your thoughts and experiences and get feedback from your readers. A V-LOG uses video. You update the content frequently – weekly, daily or even several times an hour. Setting up a blog takes less than five minutes. How much time and energy you then put into it is up to you.

You could become the voice of your community… providing the latest news, praising and criticising local officials, getting the views of election candidates on key issues… concentrating on a major issue that nobody is addressing, such as road traffic, homelessness, gangs, police brutality, so that it can no longer be ignored… becoming the expert on that issue and lobbying for change.

Set up your blog for free at *Blogger*: **www.blogger.com**
Or use *Wordpress* to put your blog on your website: **http://wordpress.org**

Download the *Handbook for Bloggers and Cyber-Dissidents* from *Reporters without Borders*. This explains how to set up a blog, publicise it (getting it picked up by search-engines) and establish its credibility. Search on *"Handbook"* at: **http://en.rsf.org**

START TWEETING

Twitter enables you to get short messages out to people in real time from your computer or cellphone. You can follow people on *Twitter* to hear what they are saying; you can also sign up on *Twitter* and get your own followers, and then send *Tweets* to them. Each message must be no longer than 140 characters.

Twitter invites you to answer these questions: *"What am I doing?"* and *"What are my thoughts on what's happening?"* in your life or in the wider world around you. You can send photos or video clips along with your message, by uploading these on sites such as *Flickr* or *YouTube* and providing the link.

Twitter has become a phenomenon in just a few years, putting the *instant* into communication. You need to get followers, of course. So ask people to follow you – on your website, at the bottom of your e-mails or when you meet them, and invite the people you follow to follow you.

You should have something to say that's of interest to others; people won't want to hear about the boring details of your daily life. You may find important well-connected people following you, and what you say being picked up or re-tweeted so your message spreads and starts to influence things. Start *Tweeting*, sign up at: **http://twitter.com**

BECOME A PODCASTER

Anyone can make an audio diary. You just need a microphone, a recorder and a pair of headphones. Recording is not difficult; you will learn as you go along. So if you or someone in your community has a story to tell or something that they want to say out loud, record it and then podcast it. If you don't know how, take the *Podcast Tutorial* at: **www.how-to-podcast-tutorial.com**

Find out about *Podcasting* at: **http://en.wikipedia.org/wiki/Podcasting**

Radio Diaries helps people produce their own oral histories: teenagers, seniors, prisoners and others whose voices are rarely heard. People are given a recorder for three months to two years to conduct interviews, keep an audio journal, and record the sounds of daily life. Find out how. Download their *"Teen Reporter Handbook"*: **http://newroutes.org/node/238**

BECOME A GURU

If you can inspire other people, you can create a movement for change. Political leaders know this. Religious leaders know this. Why shouldn't leaders of social change use similar tactics?

A guru is someone regarded as having great knowledge, wisdom and authority which they use to guide others.

To be a guru, you need followers. These ideas might help:

✳ Have a great idea which is "right for the time".

✳ Develop a charismatic personality and a "gift of the gab".

✳ Dress all in white (so you appear god-like!).

✳ Round up a few acolytes from the people you know, as these first few supporters will encourage others to join (just like Jesus did with his 12 Disciples).

✳ Get endorsed by celebrities and VIPs. This helps ordinary mortals overcome their hesitations.

✳ Provide a simple way for people to sign up.

✳ Offer some sort of "bribe" as a further inducement. But try not to pay your supporters with real money (which some political parties do), as this will make the whole thing unsustainable.

New Message   ⊖ ⊡ ⊗

File   Edit   View   Insert   Format   Tools   Message   Help

✉
Send

From: click2change@gmail.com

To:

Cc:

Subject: URLs

www.blogger.com
http://wordpress.org
http://en.rsf.org
http://twitter.com
www.how-to-podcast-tutorial.com
http://en.wikipedia.org/wiki/Podcasting
http://newroutes.org/node/238

34. SAY THANK YOU

When someone has done something good for you or good for the world, thank them. Even say it more than once, *"Thank you, thank you, thank you"*. It's really easy to do. Yet how often do we fail to do it?

So make a point of thanking people… whoever they are, whenever they deserve it. Do it right now. E-mail a letter of thanks to someone for something they have done. Here are some other ways of making someone's day. You can:

1. *Praise people… and mean it:* "I saw what you did, and it was really great!", "You're really important to me", "You're looking great"…

2. *Smile at people* – as you pass them in the street, when you are sitting opposite them in a subway or when you're stuck in a traffic jam. Smiles are infectious.

3. *Lend a hand when someone needs it.* Help an old person across the street, or someone with a pushchair trying to navigate some steps, or someone with heavy shopping. Do this without being asked.

Join the day-maker movement, doing what you can to make people's days and make the world a happier place: **www.daymakermovement.com**

THANK YOU GIFTS

The twin technologies of the internet and digital printing now make it possible to produce short-runs of t-shirts, calendars, mugs and even books at unbelievably cheap prices. Use this to create a very special thank-you gift.

1. ***Make a date of it:*** Create a personal calendar with your thank-you message on the front and 12 full-colour illustrations inside… with somebody's name in fireworks lighting up the sky, written in sand on the beach, spelt out in a topiary hedge, in the clouds, etc. It can start with any month. **www.gettingpersonal.co.uk**

2. ***Put it book:*** Collect people's reminiscences and testimonials for the person are thanking. Design it to look good and with an attractive cover. Upload this on to *Lulu* or *Blurb (Chapter 29)*; and produce a single copy to give as a thank you: **www.lulu.com**

FESTIVALS OF THANKSGIVING

Throughout history and all over the world, people have celebrated the harvest with some sort of thanksgiving ceremony.

* Demeter, the ancient Greek goddess of grain, was thanked at the festival of *Thesmosphoria*. On the first day, married women built leafy shelters. The second day was a fast day. The third was a feast with offerings to Demeter.

* The Romans had *Cerelia* on 4th October, when the fruits of the harvest were offered up to Ceres with music, parades, games and a feast.

* The Chinese harvest festival is *Chung Ch'ui*, held at full moon in the 8th month. This was the moon's birthday, celebrated with special "moon cakes", stamped with a picture of a rabbit (the Chinese see a rabbit, not a man, in the moon).

* The Jewish harvest festival is *Sukkoth*, the feast of tabernacles, when families build small huts out of branches and foliage decorated with the fruits of the harvest as a place to eat in or even sleep out in.

* The *Festival of Thanksgiving* in the USA commemorates the founding Pilgrims' first year in the New World and a plentiful harvest. It is a day of family get-togethers and turkey dinners.

SAY YOU'RE SORRY

However nice a person you are, it is almost certain there is someone you've wronged or harmed or insulted or had a huge argument with. You've probably let things get to a point where you are not speaking that person, or you may have completely lost contact with them.

You may have thought about apologising for what you have done, but you've never made enough of an effort to actually do this.

So make amends. Bury the past. Apologise. Admit responsibility. Do whatever you can to heal the situation. It will be one less thing to worry about.

Find out how to make amends: **www.wikihow.com/Make-Amends**

Make a list of everyone you would like to say sorry to or have lost contact with. Pick up the phone, write a letter… or send an email to first person on your list.

POOP SOMEONE TODAY

If you can't bring yourself to make amends, here's a way of getting your revenge on somebody. Send them a turd!

A well-known reality TV star once admitted to doing this. She was reported as saying: *"I mean, I don't just do it to anybody. They have to have done something really bad."* She sent her turd in a Tiffany box.

No smell, no dirty hands, just good clean fun – you can send a hand-sculpted ultra-realistic turd at: **www.poopprank.com**.

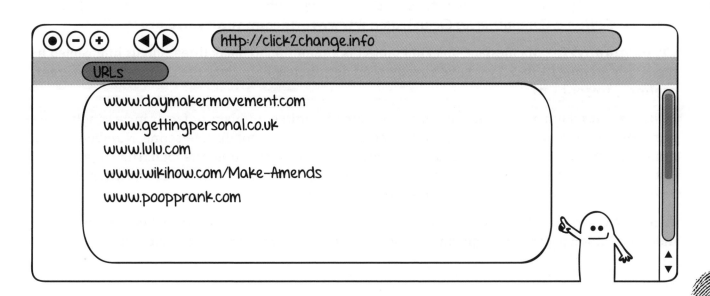

THANK YOU!

http://click2change.info

URLs

www.daymakermovement.com
www.gettingpersonal.co.uk
www.lulu.com
www.wikihow.com/Make-Amends
www.poopprank.com

35. JOIN A DISTRIBUTED NETWORK

Some problems require so much computing power, that it's impossible for any one computer, however big it is, to solve them in a reasonable period of time. But if a large number of PCs are linked together via the internet in what is called a "Distributed Network" and small parts of the problem are given to each computer, then the different bits can be combined so that the bigger problem is solved.

Distributed Network projects may involve hundreds of thousands of computers from all over the world doing such things as trying to find bigger and bigger prime numbers, creating drugs for diseases such as Alzheimers, Huntingtons, cancer and AIDS, studying evolution and a whole lot more.

Joining a *Distributed Network* is easy. You choose a project, go to its website, download some software and keep your computer turned on. Your computer will use its unused storage and processing capacity to help solve the problem whilst it's not being used by you. You won't notice anything.

So, when you have finished with your computer for the day, you could:

✳ Either harness its unused computing power. Find a project that interests you at:
http://distributedcomputing.info/projects.html

✳ Or switch it off, and save energy.

A TASTE OF WHAT'S AVAILABLE

These are some active projects:

Science: Help predict Planet Earth's climate 50 years into the future. This will be invaluable for developing policies for climate change. You can also help predict the climate in selected regions of Africa with *AfricanClimate@Home*, where arguably the impact of climate change will be more severe and communities least able to respond. **www.climateprediction.net**

Space: Search for extra-terrestrial intelligence by scanning radio signals from space. So far nobody's found anything! **http://setiathome.berkeley.edu**

Life sciences: *World Community Grid*'s mission is to create the largest public computing grid benefiting humanity. These are some of their projects: *Discovering Dengue Drugs, Human Proteome Folding, Fight AIDS@Home, Computing for Clean Water*: **www.worldcommunitygrid.org**

Cryptography: The *M4* message-breaking project is attempting to break three signals intercepted in the North Atlantic in 1942. Two have already been deciphered; help crack the third: **www.bytereef. org/m4_project.html**

Mathematics: Find a number. Many projects search for prime numbers or factor increasingly large numbers (to see what numbers multiplied together create that total). "Mersenne Numbers" are 2 multiplied by itself an increasing number of times, with 1 deducted from the total. The largest prime discovered so far is a Mersenne – 2 to the factor of 32,582,657 minus 1. Join the *Great Internet Prime Search* for an even bigger Mersenne prime: **http://mersenne.org**

Internet: Crawl the internet to see which sites have changed their content, and update a master search index of a billion pages. This might one day out-Google *Google*: **www.majestic12.co.uk**

Financial: Determine optimum stock investment strategies, and generate buy and sell signals for all major US-traded stocks by testing over a billion investment strategies for each stock using years of trading data. Beat *Goldman Sachs*, but without the bonuses: **www.gstock.com**

Art: Render images and animations for films. Check out the *Electric Sheep Project*: **www.electricsheep.org**

Puzzles and games: Play *Chess960@home*. Use distributed computing to play a variant of chess where *"the initial configuration of the chess pieces is determined randomly: that means that the king, the queen, the rook, the bishop and the knight are not necessarily placed on the same home squares"*. There are 960 possible starting positions. **www.chess-960.org/english**

Here are some more projects which are under development (they may or may not happen):
The PhotonStar Project will require a PC, an Internet connection, a Global Positioning System (GPS) receiver, and a telescope to which will be attached a laser detector to join with thousands of others to create a giant telescope, which will be used to detect laser pulses from a specific star system at a specific time. **www.photonstar.org**

NANO@Home will solve nanotechnology problems, specifically to create nanoscale equivalents of real-world parts (like bolts, screws, valves, wheels, hinges), contributing to a nano-widget library of devices from which more complex nanoscale machines could be designed. **http://boinc-wiki.info/ Nano@Home**

PlanetQuest will look for planets around other stars. **www.planetquest.org**

orbit@home will monitor the impact hazard posed by Near Earth Objects. **http://orbit.psi.edu**

Find more upcoming projects at: **http://distributedcomputing.info/upcoming.html**
Or join a fun project at **http://distributedcomputing.info/fun.html**

If you are energetic enough, you could join a project where you do the work, not your computer! You could be proofreading optically-scanned text, contributing towards a better understanding of artificial intelligence, teaching robots to become smarter, searching for interstellar stardust in a NASA sample, creating botanical information from herbarium sheets, classifying newly-discovered galaxies and much more. **http://distributedcomputing.info/ap-human.html**

Click2Change URLs
http://distributedcomputing.info/projects.html
http://setiathome.berkeley.edu
www.climateprediction.net
www.worldcommunitygrid.org
www.bytereef.org/m4_project.html
http://mersenne.org
www.majestic12.co.uk
www.gstock.com
www.electricsheep.org
www.chess-960.org/english
www.photonstar.org
http://boinc-wiki.info/Nano@Home
www.planetquest.org
http://orbit.psi.edu
http://distributedcomputing.info/upcoming.html
http://distributedcomputing.info/fun.html
http://distributedcomputing.info/ap-human.html

36. BECOME A SOCIAL NETWORKER

George Soros once famously described *"Networking"* as *"Not working"*. He saw it as an excuse to chat rather than do anything useful. But meeting people and sharing ideas can spark your creativity and lead to new ways of collaborating.

Benjamin Franklin loved chatting to friends. In 1727, he organised *"The Junto"*, a group which met on Friday evenings to discuss topics of interest. Members came from different occupations and backgrounds, but all shared a curiosity as well as a desire to improve their community and to help others. Through *The Junto*, Franklin developed such initiatives as volunteer fire-fighting clubs, improved security (night watchmen), and a public hospital.

Today we can network online as well as in the real world.

ONLINE NETWORKING

The 2000's saw the rise of social networking, which differs from real-world networking in its scale (we can come together in the millions), the speed with which information flows (virtually free and almost instantaneously), and the way it can be used to encourage positive action on matters of immediate concern.

Here are some examples how social networking is contributing to social change in the real world:

✳ Barack Obama built support and raised money as an integral feature of his 2008 Presidential campaign: www.barackobama.com

✳ Foreign students in the UK used *Facebook* to lobby HSBC against raising interest rates on student accounts – the bank was forced to withdraw its planned changes.

✳ Millions worldwide mobilised against authoritarian government and repression in Tunisia, Eqypt and other countries in 2011 using *Facebook*, *YouTube* and *Twitter*. They took to the streets, posted content and sought to "force" political change.

Lots of social networking websites have been developed. But these four are becoming dominant:

Facebook… which connects people with friends, colleagues, classmates and others who share an interest. You can communicate directly with one person (instead of sending emails) or all your friends, upload photos, share links and videos, learn more about the people you meet, and expand your network through the suggestions that *Facebook* makes for people to connect with. You can also set up or ask to join a *Facebook Group* that has been created around an issue you are passionate about. *Facebook* had over 200 million active users by the end of 2010, and is growing exponentially. **www.facebook.com**

Watch the award-winning film *"The Social Network"* about how *Facebook* was founded: **http:// thesocialnetwork-movie.com**

Google+, launched in 2011 as a rival to Facebook, which attracted 25million users in its first month and has the power of Google behind it.

Linkedin, which is a social network for professional people to connect. It has more than 100 million members in over 200 countries. **www.linkedin.com**

Twitter, where you follow other people and acquire your own followers *(see Chapter 33)*. 75 million users send 95 million *Tweets* every day. *Twitter* has become the best source of instant information when things are really happening, such as at an anti-war demonstration or when there's political unrest on the streets. **www.twitter.com**

Use **Tweetdeck** to organise your tweeting, and help you to effortlessly stay updated with the people and topics you care about. **www.tweetdeck.com**

Explore this website for lots and lots of useful ideas for ways in which you can use social media effectively: **http://www.delicious.com/day_jess/socialmedia**

USE NING TO BUILD YOUR OWN SOCIAL NETWORK

Ning provides you with the tools you need to build your very own social network around the cause or organisation you are passionate about. You can launch it in less than 60 seconds. It comes in three sizes: *Ning Mini* which is suitable for a small community of interest or a school network with up to 150 members (cost $20 per annum), *Ning Plus* for larger communities (cost $200 per annum) and *Ning Pro* which is their premium product. Features enable people to blog, share photos, view videos, join forums, chat, and use *Ning* apps and viral tools to spread the word. **www.ning.com**

BE AN ACTIVE SOCIAL NETWORKER

1. Update your profile and more photos presenting you as you really are and detailing your interests and current concerns.

2. Spread your network. Invite more of your friends, colleagues and contacts to become your *Facebook* friends or *Twitter* followers. Every time somebody invites you to connect, find two others and invite them.

3. Search your friends' friends to see if any of them have similar interests to you, and then invite them to become your friends.

4. Create a *Facebook* page around your passions, things like the environment or Quentin Tarantino's films, and find fans who are as enthusiastic as you.

5. Engage actively with your network: share resources, news, opinions, ideas, your favourite books, websites, etc.

6. But don't get stuck in virtual reality. Go and meet real friends in the real world, where people can smile and laugh together, and interact to do things together for a better world. Start a MeetUp group on an issue that excites or concerns you at **www.meetup.com**

TWEET PIE

Early in 2011, a group of people decided to crowdsource recipes over *Twitter*. They were flooded with hundreds of recipes sent in by people describing how to cook a dish in 140 characters or less. Now, the best of these have been compiled into a cookbook. *Tweet Pie* is the world's shortest recipe book. It can be bought for less than a fiver and all profits go to *FoodCycle*.

"Part social media experiment, part indispensable kitchen companion, Tweet Pie provides new and exciting dishes in the space of a single sentence."

Order *Tweet Pie* at **www.foodcycle.org.uk**

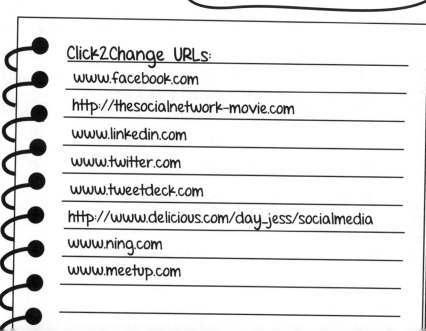

Click2Change URLs:
- www.facebook.com
- http://thesocialnetwork-movie.com
- www.linkedin.com
- www.twitter.com
- www.tweetdeck.com
- http://www.delicious.com/day_jess/socialmedia
- www.ning.com
- www.meetup.com

37. DO THE LIBRARY THING

If you have read a book and been really influenced by it, then that book might influence others… and by creating a ripple, change the whole world.

LibraryThing is a social network for book lovers. It allows you to list all your books or just the books you really love and want to tell others about. You can browse other people's book collections, trade recommendations, develop relationships with people who share your interests, find information on bookstores and book events, display a random book from your library (an *"iPod Shuffle for books"*).

To date, more than 1.2 million people have created booklists on the *LibraryThing*, posting information on more than 60 million books.

Go to the *LibraryThing* website. Search for your favourite authors to see how popular they are. Read the reviews people have written about their or your favourite books. Find out what other books those people who share your passion for a particular author or book are reading. Check out the *"Zeitgeist"* page, where you'll find the top 25 titles, top 75 authors, top 75 tag categories, and much more.

It's really easy to catalogue your books. You just enter a title or an author, and the site searches *Amazon. com* and major library sites for matching books. Then, with another click, you can add the book to your list. If you have a rare or unusual book, you add the details manually. The service is free for the first 200 books you list. If you want to list more books than that, annual membership costs $10 per annum, lifetime membership is $25.

Each time you add a book, *LibraryThing* automatically posts an image of its front cover, the date of publication, the ISBN (International Standard Book Number), other published editions, and where to buy the book online. You can add tags, a star rating, a Dewey Decimal Number, the date you acquired the book, started reading it and finished it, your own comments, or even a thoughtful review.

The site automatically generates book recommendations based on the titles in your list. It gives you a list of people who own the same books. You can track down someone who shares your tastes and request a recommendation from them, You can even ask them if a book you're thinking of buying is any good.

Sign up and start cataloguing all your books… or just your favourites… or the books that have influenced you… or books that you would recommend to people wanting to change the world. **www.librarything.com**

If you are looking for a book to read…
Type in key words such as *"Climate Change"*. Up will come a list of books by popularity. For Climate Change, the most popular books were:

1. *The Weather Makers*, Tim Flannery

2. *Field Notes from a Catastrophe*, Elizabeth Kolbert

3. *An Inconvenient Truth*, Al Gore

4. *Forty Signs of Rain*, Kim Stanley Robinson

5. *Heat*, George Monbiot

6. *Fifty Degrees Below*, Kim Stanley Robinson

Find a topic that interests you, and find books to read at: **www.librarything.com/search**

CROSS YOUR BOOKS

The internet also provides you with a way of sharing your books (but not your e-books)… through *BookCrossing*:

Is there a book which you have really enjoyed or found particularly useful, which you would like others to read? Maybe it is gathering dust on your bookshelf. So, take it off the shelf, write some comments about why you like it and why others should read it in the inside front cover. Go to the *BookCrossing* website, register the book and follow the instructions. You then leave the book somewhere for someone else to find, read and then pass on to somebody else.

The Three R's of BookCrossing

✳   *R1:* Read a good book… a book that you would recommend to others.

✳   *R2:* Register the book with *BookCrossing*. Log in your details. Get a *BookCrossing* identification number and the URL of the *BookCrossing* website. Label the book with these references, and put a note asking the reader to pass it on. Download printed labels from the *BookCrossing* website.

✳   *R3:* Release the book for someone else to read. Give it to a friend. Or leave it somewhere for someone to pick up – on a park bench, in a coffee shop… Or release it "into the wild", when people can search for it with clues you have posted on the *BookCrossing* website.

Then wait and see what happens. You will be joining 930,000 other people in 132 countries who are sharing 8 million books with the world. **www.bookcrossing.com**

SHARE YOUR BOOKS

Sutton Bookshare is a virtual library in South London, enabling people to lend and borrow books on the internet. You find a book you want to read, and arrange to pick it up. It's free, easy to use and open all local residents. Real libraries are closing down. Maybe this is an answer. **http://suttonbookshare.org.uk**

Click2Change URLs
www.librarything.com
www.librarything.com/search
www.bookcrossing.com
http://suttonbookshare.org.uk

38. SHARE YOUR WIFI AND A LOT ELSE

Apple call them *"AirPorts"*, but for most of us it's *"WiFi"*. But whether you connect wirelessly or via a modem, you really must have access to broadband to send messages, view web pages and download films and music.

A broadband connection can cost quite a lot – from around £75 to £200 per annum. But you could save much of this by sharing yours with one or two others. Once you have paid for the connection, you can add a limited number of additional users for free. All each user needs to access the connection is to register with a password.

If you want to get online you will almost certainly find that you are within range of several wireless networks. Some may not need a password, so you can just connect to them (when they are switched on, which may not be 24/7) and pay nothing at all for internet access.

If a password is required, you will have to find a way of getting it. Knock on people's doors – in your apartment block or your near neighbours – to see if they are using WiFi, and if they would be happy to share it with you (offering to pay your share the costs, of course).

Or a small group of neighbours could get together and sign up to start a new account, with the base station located in one person's apartment, and everyone else able to connect wirelessly.

So, get your broadband by starting your very own WiFi co-op. Spread the ethos of sharing and cooperation – and save money at the same time. Set up your own *AirPort*!

PLEDGE TO STOP FLYING

Whilst you are setting up your *AirPort*, why not pledge to stop flying?

Choosing to be free from air travel won't do anything for your broadband; but it will stop you rushing hither and thither, and so help reconnect you with people and places around you. It is a big step that you can take to help prevent climate change. Make a pledge at: **www.lowflyzone.org**

You can make this pledge at two levels:

* *Gold Pledge:* pledging not to travel by air for a minimum of 12 months, except in an emergency.

* *Silver Pledge:* pledging to avoid all leisure flights (but not business flights), for a minimum of 12 months.

On the *LowFlyZone* website, you can:

* *Get advice on alternative methods of travel* and read about the experiences of people who are choosing to holiday or participate in international business meetings, without flying.

* *Contribute your own experiences* of a flight-free life, and post pictures of places you have travelled to without flying.

* *Search the database* to find other people who have pledged – and to find out about their reasons for doing this.

Watch the polar bear film, and take action to stop airport expansion in the UK at **www.planestupid.org.uk**

SHARING THINGS

Sharing and cooperating with others are good for society. They are also good for the environment, as everything that is shared means one less thing to be purchased and consumed. This is called "Collaborative Consumption". Read the book *"What's Mine is Yours"*: **http://collaborativeconsumption.com** and check out this website: **http://thepeoplewhoshare.com**

THEN SHARE THIS BOOK WITH OTHERS

After you have read *"What's Mine is Yours"*, then do one of these things:

* Pass it on to a friend to read.

* Register it on *Bookcrossing* and leave it for someone else to pick up and read *(Chapter 37)*: **www.bookcrossing.com**

* Donate it to a public library.

* Sell it on *Amazon*.

SOME OTHER THINGS YOU CAN SHARE

* *Share your children's toys.* Pass them on to another child when they are no longer being used, or donate them to a toy library or to a children's hospital.

* *Share a ride* (this is sometimes called "carpooling"), and halve the number of journeys you take. You will be reducing congestion as well as pollution. Share a ride if you're driving somewhere. Find a ride if you need someone to take you, Sign up at: **www.liftshare.com**

* *Share a bath* or a shower with a friend and halve your water use. Splash around and enjoy.

* *Share one side of a sheet of paper* with the other. Print double sided. Use the blank reverse side of paper that has already been printed on.

* *Share your bicycle.* Ride a Boris Bike. Or ride a tandem… it's much less effort and a lot of fun – provided you both want to go the same way!

* *Share a joke.* Make somebody laugh and help create a happier world. If you can find a good joke-a-day website, subscribe to it.

* *Share your house* when you're travelling through **www.airbnb.com**

* *Share your couch* with travellers or go couchsurfing at **www.couchsurfing.net**

www.lowflyzone.org
www.planestupid.org.uk
http://collaborativeconsumption.com
http://thepeoplewhoshare.com
www.bookcrossing.com
www.liftshare.com
www.airbnb.com
www.couchsurfing.net

39. ORGANISE A DINNER OF HOPE

Organising a dinner is a good way of raising money for a good cause. But organising a big dinner can be extremely risky. You have to pay out a lot of money just for the venue and the caterer; and there are other large up-front expenses too.

Hosting a dinner in your own home is a much cheaper and much less risky alternative. You can invite your friends, download recipes, and order the food all from your computer. Your guests turn up, eat, enjoy themselves and are asked to make a donation.

Host a dinner for a cause you feel passionate about or to mark *Earth Day* or *Thanksgiving*. Invite a dozen or so people. Cook and pay for the dinner yourself as your contribution. What your guests contribute goes to your chosen cause.

Organising your dinner: These are the steps you need to take.

1. Decide on the cause you are raising money for.

2. Fix a date and time.

3. Decide the theme for the dinner – a dinner for the Ecuadorian rainforest might have a South American-themed menu.

4. Write the invitation. Make the dinner seem a lot of fun; but mention its purpose and suggest a minimum contribution (almost certainly less than the cost of a meal out).

5. E-mail your invitation to around 30 people. You could also ask your friends abroad to organise their own dinners.

6. Wait for the replies. Telephone people if they don't respond. If too many people accept, it may be a bit of a crush – but you'll raise lots more money!

7. Decide what you are going to eat and drink. Order the ingredients online.

8. Cook the dinner. Lay the table.

9. Enjoy the dinner.

10. Make a short presentation about the cause. Ask people to put their contributions in an envelope (which you provide).

And finally, encourage your guests to organise their own dinner – start a *"Chain Dinner"*.

LUNCHES AND DINNERS TO INSPIRE YOU

The Big Lunch: This UK event is a one-day get-together for neighbours, It can take place anywhere – in the street, a park, somebody's garden, at a school. Almost 1 million people take part each year. The website has guidance on how to organise it, menus and recipes, and what entertainment to provide. **www.thebiglunch.com**

Chain dinners: The *Global Fund for Women* encouraged its supporters to organise a "chain dinner", inviting twelve people to dinner and charging them $12 each. Two guests were persuaded to invite twelve more people to another dinner at their home, again at $12 each… each of these persuaded two more people to organise a dinner… and so on. The income multiplies. The original dinner: $12 x 12 = $144. The next two dinners: 2 x $12 x 12 = $288. The next four dinners: 4 x $12x 12 = $576… Of course, not everyone who agrees to host a dinner will actually do so; and like all chains it eventually peters out. The Fund now asks its supporters to *Host a House Party*. **www.globalfundforwomen.org**

An evening of music: Daniel Pearl was an American journalist investigating the links between fundamentalism and terrorism in Pakistan. In January 2002, he was captured and beheaded. The video of his beheading was circulated by his murderers and shocked the world. In memory of Danny and to celebrate his love of music and commitment to tolerance, his widow Mariane created *Daniel Pearl Music Days*. Concerts are organised around the world during the first half of October each year (10th October was Danny's birthday). More than 1,000 events are organised in over 100 countries – from folk singers and small amateur bands to international rock stars, drum ensembles and big symphony orchestras. **www.danielpearlmusicdays.org**

ORGANISE A HUNGER BANQUET

If you are fighting hunger, it would be completely inappropriate to overeat at a big dinner. So *Oxfam America* developed the idea of a *Hunger Banquet*. Each person attending is randomly assigned a role mirroring the distribution of wealth and poverty in the world. This determines what they eat.

✳   15% are high-income; they sit at table and enjoy a three-course meal with wine and all the trimmings.

✳   25% are middle-income; they sit on chairs and eat rice and beans (delicious and nutritious!).

✳   The remaining 60% are the world's poor; they sit on the floor, and get only rice and water. They will suffer the fate of the billions of poor people throughout the world who go to bed hungry each night.

Instructions and downloads for your *Hunger Banquet*:
http://actfast.oxfamamerica.org/index.php/events/banquet

Find out more about hunger in the world and also about all the food wasted at:
www.worldhunger.org and **http://en.wikipedia.org/wiki/Food_waste**

Remember that in a hungry world with a growing population – 7 billion and counting – we can either grow more or waste less. Which is better for the environment?

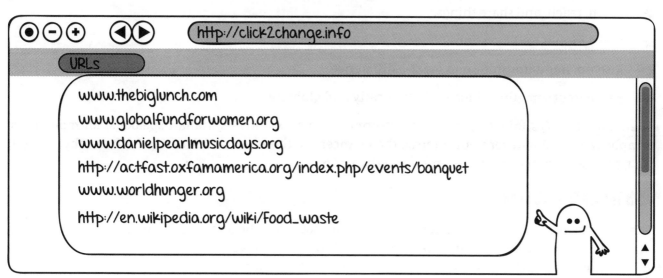

http://click2change.info

URLs

www.thebiglunch.com
www.globalfundforwomen.org
www.danielpearlmusicdays.org
http://actfast.oxfamamerica.org/index.php/events/banquet
www.worldhunger.org
http://en.wikipedia.org/wiki/Food_waste

40. MEET UP WITH OTHERS

Most of us want to do something to make the world a better place. But it can be lonely and quite hard if we just do it all by ourselves. So why not use the internet to meet up with others to change the world? The power of numbers will make it easier to achieve more than any one person on their own can. And it can be a lot more fun doing things together. This is the week to get out into the real world!

HAVE A GREEN DRINK

Every month in 793 cities all over the world people with an interest in the environment meet up through *Green Drinks* and have a beer, a glass of wine or an orange juice.

Green Drinks is *"an organic, self-organising network with a lively mixture of people from NGOs, academia, government and business, as well as people with a passion for doing something or some crazy idea they want to talk about.* Turn up and just say *"Are you green?"* and you will be introduced to whoever is there. You can test out your own ideas, or be inspired by others.

If there isn't a *Green Drinks* group near you, why not set one up? **www.greendrinks.org**

MEET UP WITH OTHERS

People can change their personal world, or even the whole world, by organising themselves in groups that are large and powerful enough to make a difference. *MeetUp* helps people set up groups around a common interest come together.

There are now 250,000 monthly meet-ups on more than 46,000 topics in 45,000 cities and towns around the world. *MeetUp* groups meet regularly in cafes, restaurants, living rooms or anywhere. Join a *MeetUp* group and…

* Meet others who share your interests.

* Get involved locally.

* Learn, teach, and share things.

* Make friends and have fun.

* Rise up, stand up, unite, and make a difference.

* Be a part of something bigger – both locally and globally.

There are *MeetUps* for everyone – Stay-at-home moms, Dog lovers, Italian speakers, Entrepreneurs, Scrapbookers… Whatever your interest, the chances are there's a local *MeetUp* for it nearby. If there isn't, then start your own group. **www.meetup.com**

JOIN THE MANIFESTO CLUB

The *Manifesto Club* began in London in London in 2006, with the aim of challenging the bureaucracy that stifles initiative and restrains creativity. The club's principles are:

1. Commitment to freedom, free speech and genuine tolerance.

2. Support for experimentation in all forms.

3. Individual self-determination.

4. Humanity and enlightenment.

The *Manifesto Club* gives you the opportunity to speak out and share ideas. Campaigns have included the freedom to fly, the removal of over-zealous child protection practices, sharing ideas on education policies and practice, and promoting greater freedom in the arts. **www.manifestoclub.com**

ACT FOR LOVE

Change the world and meet your match! *"Act for Love is an online dating service for activists, leftists, news junkies – people with brains who actually care about the world. This is the place to take action AND get action. Get started now!"*

You need to have progressive values and be single (and also live in the USA). If you do, then join the *Act for Love* network. You never know. Today might just be your lucky day! **http://actforlove.org**

MEET PEOPLE AND HAVE FUN

Here are some other ways of using the internet to get together:

* **Critical mass:** An impromptu event to celebrate cycling where cyclists just appear on the street and cycle round together enjoying the evening – and jamming up the traffic. **http://critical-mass.info** and **http://criticalmass.wikia.com**

* **Flashmobs:** A sudden gathering of people into a crowd who do something unusual in unison for a few minutes and then quickly disperse. **www.flashmob.co.uk**

* **Mobile clubbing:** Discos where people meet in public places and dance to music on their own mp3 players for a short time before dispersing. **www.mobile-clubbing.com**

* **Pillow fight clubs:** Massive pillow fights organised in public places, sometimes just for fun and sometimes to try to break a *Guinness World Record*. The fights can last from a few minutes to several hours. There's even a semi-professional women's sports league in Canada for pillow fighting. *International Pillow Fight Day* is at the beginning of April: **www.pillowfightday.com**

Click2Change URLs
www.greendrinks.org
www.meetup.com
www.manifestoclub.com
http://actforlove.org
http://critical-mass.info
http://criticalmass.wikia.com
www.flashmob.co.uk
www.mobile-clubbing.com
www.pillowfightday.com
http://en.wikipedia.org/wiki/Subway-party
www.zombiewalk.com/forum/index.php

* **Subway parties:** A party held on a mass transit system. People meet up at a predetermined station, wait until enough people have turned up, and then board the train, where there is music, dancing and sometimes the exchange of gifts. **http://en.wikipedia.org/wiki/Subway_party**

* **Zombie walks:** a walk through streets, shopping centres ending up at the local cemetery, with people dressed up in zombie costume and communicating only as zombies might – grunting, groaning and calling for "brains". **www.zombiewalk.com/forum/index.php**

41. STOP BEING RIPPED OFF

"Learn how to avoid ripoffs – send $5." – an ad in *National Enquirer* magazine

If you are being treated unfairly, or receiving an unacceptably poor level of service, or being ripped off financially, don't just sit there in silence. Do something. Find out who is responsible, and force them to do something about it. You may be able to obtain redress; you will be showing that what they are providing is unacceptable; and you may find ways of joining with others to make things better for everybody.

These are some basic rules for complaining:

* *Know exactly what you want.* This might be compensation, an apology, or changes to the procedures.

* *Have evidence* to back up your complaint

* *Deal with the person who has the power* to do something. Go right to the top if necessary.

* *Be persistent.* Don't give up – if you have a good case, you should end up winning.

* *Try to get publicity* whenever this might help.

FIGHTING FOR CONSUMER RIGHTS

The *Consumers' Association* (now known as *Which?*) started in 1957 with a magazine published from a converted garage in East London. 10,000 people subscribed in the first month. Today it is the largest consumer body in the UK with over 650,000 members.

Which? provides reports based on product testing and feedback from its members on a wide range of consumer products. It also campaigns on issues such as bank charges, cosmetic treatments, health care standards and payment protection insurance. It tackles specific issues when the need arises, such as hospital car park charges and the rights of air passengers. **www.which.co.uk**

RIP OFF BRITAIN

"My aim is to ensure that 'Rip-Off Britain' remains ingrained in our mind-set by reminding people to be more vigilant in their purchases and everyday dealings. However, if you do unfortunately get 'ripped-off', you're going to discover that by complaining effectively you'll achieve a satisfactory outcome and a result in your favour in the majority of cases." – Paul Meyer, who ran this website until 2009. See his 12 *Golden Rules* for not being ripped off. **www.rip-off.co.uk**

DON'T BE RIPPED OFF BY THE BANKS

Martin Lewis is the *"Money Saving Expert"*. He is a journalist who had his own TV series *"Make Me Rich"*, and his book *"Money Diet"* became a bestseller. He created the free, independent and ad-free *MoneySavingExpert.com* website in 2003. It is now the UK's biggest money site, covering credit cards, shopping, phones, utilities, savings and investments. Loans and banking, insurance, travel and transport, mortgages and homes.

Take a tour of *MoneySavingExpert.com,* play the money saving game, sign up for the newsletter, and do one thing to get yourself a better deal: **www.moneysavingexpert.com**

See the 50 word suggestions for making life fairer when dealing with companies and financial matters submitted to the website, which aims to be a *"Moneyfesto"* for consumer rights.

SAY NO TO 0870

Premium lines are often the basis for a rip off. In 2007, UK broadcasters were called to account rigging phone-in competitions where callers paid high charges (shared between the broadcaster and the telecoms operator) for ringing in answers in the hope that they might win a prize.

But there are other ways in which we are being ripped off through premium lines. When you telephone a company to complain or ask for advice, you often have to ring a 0844, 0845, 0870 or 0871 number, and you may be charged a rip-off rate instead of just paying the local or national rate.

The company might give people calling from abroad a different number (this will begin with the country code +44). There is nothing to stop you using this from the UK (when you will be charged a normal rate). Sometimes the company will give you a standard number if you ask.

The *sayNOto0870* website lists alternative numbers. Use this to see if there is a cheaper number – just enter the company name or the high-rate number. If you discover cheaper numbers for a company, you can add these to the website, so others can save money. You can join the (current) campaign against these numbers – which GPs and out-of-hours medical services are also starting to use. **www.saynoto0870.com**

ANOTHER WAY OF COMPLAINING...

Form a *Complaints Choir*. Make a list of all your complaints, set this to music, and sing them (preferably in public or on the radio, with as much publicity as you can get)! People all over the world have done this. It started in Birmingham, then in Helsinki, St Petersburg and Hamburg. Read the *"Nine-Step Guide to Organising a Complaints Choir"*: **www.complaintschoir.org**

www.which.co.uk
www.rip-off.co.uk
www.moneysavingexpert.com
www.saynoto0870.com
www.complaintschoir.org

42. JOIN A RAPID RESPONSE NETWORK

The internet allows information to spread around the world in a flash. No longer do letters have to be written, put in an envelope, stamped and posted, arriving days or weeks later… which is why this way of communicating is referred to as *"Snail Mail"*. Now you can write an e-mail, and with a click it will arrive instantaneously.

Rapid Response Networks enable thousands or even hundreds of thousands of people to be mobilised whenever an urgent issue arises. You receive alerts asking you to e-mail someone to show your concern or suggest what needs to be done. This can be a letter you write yourself, or it might be a standard letter which you edit to include a few of your own words, or you might just be asked to insert your name and e-mail address and click to send.

There are *Rapid Response Networks* for all sorts of issues. So if a journalist is apprehended in pursuit of the truth, a flood of letters can be sent immediately demanding her release. Or if a politician uses homophobic language, he can receive thousands of protest letters.

These letters may not actually be read, and might be seen as "Spam". But if somebody receives a flood of letters, it must make them rethink the issue.

AMNESTY'S URGENT ACTION NETWORK

If you are concerned about human rights, then join Amnesty's *Urgent Action Network*. You will be alerted when immediate public pressure is needed to try to protect a prisoner from torture, medical neglect, unfair trial, a judicial death penalty, extra-judicial execution or forcible repatriation.

You could make an impact on someone like *Kamal al-Labwani*, a doctor and pro-democracy activist, sentenced to 12 years imprisonment following an unfair trial on the trumped up charge of *"plotting or scheming with a foreign country, or communicating with one, with the aim of causing it to attack Syria"*. Or *Lema Susarov*, a Chechen refugee, whom the Ukrainian authorities wanted to forcibly return to the Russian Federation, where he would be at serious risk of torture. It needs just a few moments of your time. Sign up at: **www.amnesty.org/en/activism-center**. And at: **www.amnesty.org.uk**

Where you can also add an *Amnesty* widget to your *Facebook* profile to encourage your friends to take action, and send greetings cards to prisoners with messages of support and hope.

TIPS FOR LETTER WRITING

✱ *Speed is vital* for urgent action.

✱ *Letters should be brief, factual and polite*, giving accurate details of the situation.

✱ Write as if the reader is *open to reasoned argument*.

✱ *Make a clear request.*

✱ Say a little about yourself to *show why you are concerned*.

✱ *Write in English* unless you can get an accurate translation.

✱ Use *a conclusion that encourages a reply*.

✱   If you are sending a letter by post, it can be *hand-written or typed.*

Amnesty's letter-writing tips: **www.amnesty.org.uk/content.asp?CategoryID=949**

SIGN UP TO AVAAZ

Avaaz involves over 10 million people from around the world in making their voice heard to key global decision-makers, corporations and the media on issues such as climate change, conflict and world poverty. Sign up to receive emails and text messages which alert you to new campaigns and opportunities for both online and off-line action.

Avaaz decides its campaign issues by polling its members. The top three issues are environment/climate change, human rights (including torture, genocide and trafficking), and poverty, disease and development: **www.avaaz.org**

A 38-degree slope is the tipping point at which a snowfall turns into an avalanche. *38 Degrees* is a UK-based rapid response network for social and environmental justice: **http://38degrees.org.uk**

In Australia, there's *GetUp*: **www.getup.org.au**

SET UP YOUR OWN RAPID RESPONSE NETWORK

You can set up your own *Rapid Response Network* on an issue that concerns you. This could be a very local issue, such as potholes in the streets, or an important national or international issue. Just find others who share your concern, and then alert them whenever a letter needs to be sent, providing them with a draft and the name and e-mail address of the person to send it to.

Posted on *PledgeBank.com*: *"I will set up and run a new urgent action network for Tibet but only if 100 other people will sign up to receive regular email actions for Tibet."* – David Meanwell. 118 people signed up to this. The *Tibet Urgent Response Network* brings together activists prepared to write, phone and email governments, MPs, businesses and media on the Chinese occupation and human rights abuses in Tibet. Find out more at: **www.causes.com/causes/314261-tibet-urgent-response-network**

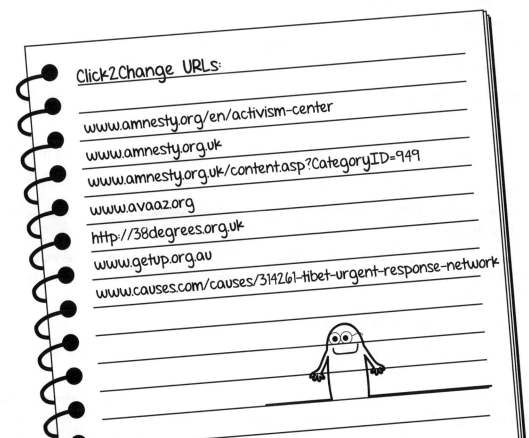

Click2Change URLs:

www.amnesty.org/en/activism-center
www.amnesty.org.uk
www.amnesty.org.uk/content.asp?CategoryID=949
www.avaaz.org
http://38degrees.org.uk
www.getup.org.au
www.causes.com/causes/314261-tibet-urgent-response-network

43. SEND AN ONLINE PETITION

One good way of gathering support for an idea or an issue is to organise a petition. If you can get lots of people to sign this, it will demonstrate the strength and depth of public feeling that something needs to be done.

You no longer need to go house to house knocking on people's doors to talk to people and ask them to sign up. This is hard work and takes a lot of time. It is far simpler to put your petition online, and then email all your contacts asking them to support it.

Here are two websites for organising a petition:
>The Petition Site: **www.thepetitionsite.com/create.html**
>PetitionOnline: **www.petitiononline.com**

But before you do anything, you should first decide:

✱ *What's the big issue* or big idea around which you want to mobilise public support.

✱ *Who your petition is aimed at…* and what do you want them to do.

✱ *How many signatures you want*, how you will reach people who might be interested, and how you will persuade them of the importance of the issue.

Once you have thought through all of this, compose your petition, put it online and try to get 100 or 1,000 or even 100,000 people to sign up as supporters. Once you are starting to attract support, send your petition to politicians, companies, journalists and opinion formers – to whoever can help you get the change you are seeking – to bring the issue to their attention and explore with them how they might support you.

What makes a good petition?

✱ It clearly explains the issue and what change you are seeking.

✱ It provides concrete facts to substantiate your point of view.

✱ It is brief – normally no longer than half a page.

How to collect lots of signatures:

✱ Send e-mails to your friends giving the URL of your online petition and asking them to sign up.

✱ Post links on relevant discussion boards.

✱ Contact writers and journalists who write about the topic to tell them about your petition, and ask them to publicise it.

✱ Send out a press release announcing your petition, but only do this once you have obtained enough signatures to show that public support exists or when you have recruited some high-profile signatories.

✱ Add a link to your petition in your e-mail signature and on your web site.

✱ Ask special interest groups with large audiences to add a link on their website or in their newsletters.

✱ Submit your petition page to search engines (it usually takes between 3 and 4 weeks to be indexed). Type into Google *"submit search engines"* to find a way of reaching a lot of search engines for free.

SOME POPULAR ONLINE PETITIONS

To the Prime Minister of Japan: to stop the annual brutal slaughter of dolphins and whales that takes place in Japan.

To the UK government: to save 10 UK coastguard centres threatened with closure due to government cuts in the interests of maritime safety.

To the Government of the Islamic Republic of Iran: for the immediate release of internationally respected and award-winning Iranian Filmmaker Jafar Pahani.

To UNESCO: to recognise the Tomb of the Patriarchs in Hebron as a World Heritage Site.
[All from the PetitionOnline website]

PETITION THE PRIME MINISTER OR THE PRESIDENT

The UK Prime Minister's *10 Downing Street* website once provided a *Petition-the-Prime-Minister* facility for you to get your petition directly to the Prime Minister's office and possibly to his personal attention: **www.number-10.gov.uk**. This service was launched in November 2006, but has since ceased. It has been replaced by a government e-petition service. You can create an e-petition about anything that the government is responsible for; if it gets 100,000 signatures, it is eligible for debate in the House of Commons. **http://epetitions.direct.gov.uk**

Ask the White House allowed you to interact with Bush administration officials. Citizens were able to participate in online discussions with Cabinet Secretaries, Senior White House Officials, behind-the-scenes professionals at the White House, and others. The Obama White House launched an *Open for Questions* pilot scheme for people to ask a question and vote on its importance, and they are looking for new ways to engage the public: **www.whitehouse.gov/openforquestions**

It is too easy for our political leaders to create one-way channels for communicating information outwards, rather than mechanisms for getting feedback and entering into discussions on issues of public concern. The internet offers amazing possibilities for politicians to connect and interact, and not just when they want your vote!

There's nothing to stop you from writing anyway to your Prime Minister or President on any issue that particularly concerns you, or from organising your own online petition to bring the issue to public attention and show the strength of public opinion, or from creating a petition asking your elected representative to listen more and speak less!

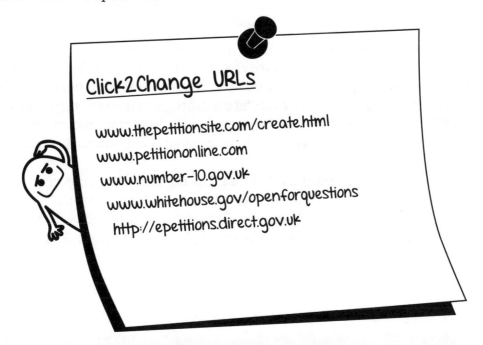

Click2Change URLs

www.thepetitionsite.com/create.html
www.petitiononline.com
www.number-10.gov.uk
www.whitehouse.gov/openforquestions
http://epetitions.direct.gov.uk

44. FIGHT CENSORSHIP

Freedom of expression is widely seen as a fundamental human right for all humanity. Those countries which have signed the *Universal Declaration of Human Rights* have formally accepted this. But in some countries, this freedom is denied. Play a part in fighting censorship. Make your mouse roar!

Books and other information can be censored for a variety of reasons, including politics, terrorism, public morality, religion... If you want to take a stand on freedom of expression, the best way of beating censorship is to circulate banned information as widely as you can – to all your contacts, on your website, in your blog. Ask people to pass the information on through their own networks; this is an extremely simple action that anyone can take to fight censorship.

In the 1970s and 1980s, *Samizdat Publishing* was an important dissident activity in the Soviet Union. Individuals reproduced censored publications (including work by Nobel laureate Alexander Solzhenitzin) making handwritten copies and passing these on from reader to reader. This enabled banned material to be circulated widely, and it helped build resistance which eventually led to the collapse of the regime.

In 2008, *Amnesty International* as part of its *Irrepressible* internet censorship campaign gave its supporters a badge that they could put on their website which enabled visitors to the website to view and read banned information.

For information on banned publications, go to:
International Pen: **www.pen-international.org**
Index on Censorship: **www.indexoncensorship.org**
And take a look at this list of banned books through the ages. How many of them have you read?
http://onlinebooks.library.upenn.edu/banned-books.html

FIGHT INTERNET CENSORSHIP

The internet allows us to make facts public, share our ideas, participate in collaborative activity, say what we want to whom we want. It offers us almost total freedom of expression. There will always be some restrictions on its use for good reasons – circulating child pornography, restricting young people from viewing unsuitable matter, filtering out spam, for example.

But countries such as China, Vietnam, Iran, Saudi Arabia, Afghanistan and Syria see unrestricted access to the internet as a threat. They try to monitor chat rooms, delete blogs, block websites, restrict what search engines come up with, punish people for downloading certain material. Citizens are being persecuted and imprisoned, and sometimes even face a death sentences for such acts as criticising their government, calling for democratic rights and greater press freedom, exposing human rights abuses, downloading and circulating what governments see as offensive or subversive material.

Censorship in the People's Republic of China: The *Golden Shield Project* run by the Ministry of Public Security is part of what has come to be known as the *Great Firewall of China*, which restricts access in mainland China (but not in Macau or Hong Kong) to selected websites. Find out more at:
http://en.wikipedia.org/wiki/Internet_censorship_in_the_People's_Republic_of_China

COMMONLY-USED CENSORSHIP METHODS

These are some of the techniques used for censoring internet content:

* *Blocking* a particular server and all the websites it hosts.

* *Domain Name Server (DNS) filtering* and redirection.

* *Uniform Resource Locator (URL) filtering*, blocking certain web addresses.

* *Packet filtering*, when certain controversial keywords are detected.

* *Connection reset.* If a previous TCP connection is blocked by the filter, future connection attempts from both sides will also be blocked for up to 30 minutes.

* *Web feed blocking*, where incoming URLs starting with the words "rss", "feed", or "blog" are blocked.

* *Reverse surveillance*, where computers accessing certain websites are reverse scanned to try to extract further information from them.

GETTING AROUND CENSORSHIP

Just as quickly as the censors develop blocking techniques, so those opposing censorship develop ways around the block. Check these out:

The Great Firewall of China: This provides a tool for people to see if a domain name is censored in China. It then allowed people then to view the domain via a proxy server, but it has been taken off line because counter-measures were affecting its reliability: **www.greatfirewallofchina.org**

Psiphon: This is an "anonymizer tool" designed by *Citizen Lab* in Toronto that attempts to make internet activity untraceable. It accesses the internet on the user's behalf, protecting personal information by hiding the source computer's identifying information. Find out more, or become a *Psiphon Host*: **http://psiphon.ca**

Freegate: This programme makes visiting overseas websites as fast as visiting local ones. It has helped millions of internet users in China to access the internet faster and more stably. **http://download. cnet.com/Freegate/3000-2085_4-10415391.html**

Wikileaks: This states its mission as *"We are of assistance to peoples of all countries who wish to reveal unethical behavior in their governments and institutions. We disclose documents that are classified, censored or otherwise opaque to the public record."* **www.wikileaks.info**

Click2Change URLs

www.pen-international.org

www.indexoncensorship.org

http://onlinebooks.library.upenn.edu/banned-books.html

http://en.wikipedia.org/wiki/Internet_censorship_in_the_People's_Republic_of_China

www.greatfirewallofchina.org

http://psiphon.ca

http://download.cnet.com/Freegate/3000-2085_4-10415391.html

www.wikileaks.info

45. CAMPAIGN FROM YOUR BEDROOM

Jean-Paul Marat, a leader of the 1789 French Revolution, spent most of the time in the bath as he had a skin disease which immersion in water seemed to soothe. If Marat could run the French revolution from his bathroom, then you can surely campaign to change the world from your bedroom or study – with the help, of course, of a computer and the internet. To do this, you will need:

✳   An issue you strongly believe in.

✳   Accurate up-to-date information about this issue.

✳   Clear objectives – who you want to influence and what change you want to achieve.

✳   People who are prepared to support you.

✳   Simple and effective things for your supporters to do.

✳   Lots of publicity, so as to keep the issue in the public eye.

✳   Money – which you can ask your supporters to give or raise for you.

That's all there is to it! So think of an issue. Get started with your campaign right now.

CAMPAIGNING ON FACEBOOK

Facebook provides a useful mechanism for running a campaign. You can set out your campaign goals, share information, ask people to do things and invite feedback. Your page can include:

✳   Campaign details – all the facts and what you aim to achieve.

✳   Photographs.

✳   Who and how many people are supporting you.

✳   Latest news and announcements.

✳   A "wall of information" posted by you and your supporters.

✳   Links to:
        A fundraising page for your supporters to contribute funds.
        Newsletters, podcasts, videos, blog posts and published articles.
        Organisations and publications that relate to your cause.

There are two ways of using *Facebook* as a platform for your campaign:
1. Set up a *Facebook* Group: **www.facebook.com**
2. Use Causes: **http://nonprofits.causes.com**

"Causes provides effective tools for activists on Facebook to build communities of supporters, conduct fundraising campaigns, circulate petitions, build volunteer capacity, and more. The tools are free and allow nonprofits to empower their supporters to take action, get friends involved, and expand their reach through their social networks."

Can this Orang-Utan get more friends than Nestle? Nestlé makes products such as *KitKat*. They purchase palm oil from companies that are replacing Indonesian rainforests with palm tree planta-tions, and this is pushing the Orang-Utan towards extinction. *"We all deserve to have a break – but* *this shouldn't involve taking a bite out of Indonesia's precious rainforests. We're asking Nestlé to give rainforests and Orang-Utans a break and stop buying palm oil from destroyed forests."*

Nestlé had 90,000 fans. The campaign aimed to get more people than this to sign up as Orang-Utan fans. 25,000 signed in the first month. **www.facebook.com/group.php?gid=105561609471810**

How to buy palm-free alternatives: **www.orangutans.com.au/Orangutans-Survival-Information/Helping-you-buy-responsibly-Palm-oil-free-alternatives.aspx**

SEVEN CAMPAIGNING TIPS

1. Have *a memorable web address.*

2. *Build an e-mailing list,* and e-mail your supporters regularly with up-to-the-moment information.

3. *Have an e-postcard* that encourages your supporters to spread the word.

4. *Optimise your chances of people finding* you when they search. Useful tips: **www.searchengineoptimising.com/seo-guide**; or Google *"Google SEO Guide"* and see what comes up.

5. *Build links to lots of other organisations.*

6. *Use online directories, newsgroups and blogs* to promote your campaign.

7. Find resources on *FairSay* and join the informed, helpful and supportive *eCampaigning Forum* network. See: **http://fairsay.com**

TWO THINGS TO DO WITHOUT LEAVING HOME

Arrest yourself for Burma: If you're concerned about human rights in Burma, then *Arrest Yourself for Burma Day.* This campaign started when Aung San Suu Kyi, opposition leader and Nobel laureate, was under house arrest (she was released in 2010), to celebrate her birthday on 19th June and draw attention to the Burmese situation. This is how to organise an *"Arrest Yourself"* party:

✳ Stay home for 24 hours on 19th June, just as if you were under house arrest.

✳ During this time, host a "house arrest" party; invite friends and family to join you for a couple of hours. Cook and enjoy a Burmese meal.

✳ Screen a documentary on Burma to show your guests what's happening. Ask them to sign a petition and to contribute funds to the Burma campaign.

US Campaign for Burma: **www.uscampaignforburma.org**. Aung San Suu Kyi's website: **www.dassk.com**

Organise a Love-In for Peace: *"I'm just a normal person who lies in bed and protests against war. I'm not a hippy; I'm not a member of CND; I'm not a member of anything. But the issue is very serious, and you've got to make a stand sometime.* On the eve of the Iraq war on Valentine's Day 2003, Andrew and Christine Gale decided to stage a John & Yoko-style *Love-In* in their tiny bedroom so as to make Valentine's Day a day of love and peace. Find out more about the *Love-in Couple* and how Yoko Ono got involved **www.bbc.co.uk/videonation/person/gale_andrew**

www.facebook.com
http://nonprofits.causes.com
www.facebook.com/group.php?gid=105561609471810
www.orangutans.com.au/Orangutans-Survival-Information/Helping-you-buy-responsibly-Palm-oil-free-alternatives.aspx
www.bbc.co.uk/videonation/person/gale_andrew

www.searchengineoptimising.com/seo-guide
www.uscampaignforburma.org
http://fairsay.com
www.dassk.com

46. MAKE A PLEDGE

A pledge is a promise you make to do something. It's best if it's something specific and within a stated period of time. Otherwise it will be hard to know when you have achieved your pledge. Pledging to do something that you would do anyway or something you enjoy is easy. But for something difficult that requires a sustained effort, making a pledge can be a way of ensuring you to do it.

Pledge today to do something small each day that will make the world a little better. For example:

✳ *Join the Litter Movement*, when you pledge to do two things – to pick up one piece of litter a day and recruit at least one more person as a member. If you do this, the world will become that bit cleaner. **http://koti.welho.com/jpeltora/littermovement.htm**

✳ *Give up bottled water*. Drinking bottled water generates carbon emissions and creates congestion and pollution, whilst tap is freely available and free. Buy a water filter or a water bottle with a built in filter if you are worried about water quality. A no-brainer! **www.wewanttap.com**

STICK TO YOUR PLEDGE

Whatever you pledge to do, try to make sure that you stick to your pledge and do what you promised. This website will help you. At *stickk.com* you can create a support network to help you achieve what you pledged to do, as well as giving yourself rewards and punishments for success or failure: **www. stickk.com**

PLEDGE WITH OTHERS

If you think that the problems of the world are huge, and you what impact could just one individual make… then think about a mosquito. If this tiny insect gets into your bedroom at night, it will have a huge impact on your comfort and wellbeing. What if there were 10 or even 100 hungry mosquitoes circling around you with their incessant whine? Your life would become an absolute hell!

In just the same way, your small attempts to change the world will make some difference. But you will multiply your impact if you get lots of other people to do the same things.

So, let's say you want to switch to Green Electricity. Instead of just doing it all by yourself, why not make a pledge to do this only once you have found 9 or 99 other people who also agree to switch. Having made your pledge, your task is then to find those 9 or 99 other people.

The *PledgeBank* website helps you to this. You pledge to do something, but you only do it if a stated number of other people also pledge do the same. You find most of the people yourself, but a few visitors to the website will sign up if your pledge is interesting enough. Start by going to *Pledgebank* and sign up to someone else's pledge. **www.pledgebank.com**

Then think of something that needs doing, and post your own pledge. Decide the number of people you have to recruit before your pledge is activated. Persuade as many people as you can to join with you – everyone in your address book, your social networking fans and friends. Stick a leaflet through neighbours' doors, and even ask complete strangers you meet at parties, at meetings, or in the bus queue. Make sure you achieve your target. Exceed it if possible.

TIPS FOR SUCCESSFUL PLEDGES

(1.) *Keep your ambitions modest* — why try for 50 people when 10 would be enough? Every extra person makes your pledge harder to achieve.

(2.) *Make sure that your pledge makes sense.* Read it to someone. If they don't understand it, rewrite it.

(3.) Make your pledge seem *imaginative, worthwhile, fun…* and reasonably easy to complete.

(4.) Don't imagine that your pledge will sell itself. *You must tell the world.* You must get publicity for it.

Here are some examples of successful pledges:

✱ **To make people happy:** "I will give hugs to at least 3 people every day for a month, because I believe that the first step to world peace is showing love and compassion, but only if 10 other people in Seattle will promise to do the same." *Thirteen people signed up (three over target) to spread happiness.*

✱ **To start a campaign:** "I will campaign to Save The Sycamore (in Kingston near London), but only if 5 other local people do the same." *Five people signed up, enabling the campaign to get started.*

✱ **To get volunteer proofreaders:** Jeff edited 100 pages for *Distributed Proofreaders* once 50 other people had signed up to do the same at **www.pgdp.net**

✱ **To reduce carbon emissions:** Andy replaced all the light bulbs in his house with low-energy bulbs once 20 other people had signed up.

✱ **To get people to shop locally:** Ellie did all her shopping locally and *NOT* in a supermarket along with the 20 other people who signed up.

Click2Change URLs:

http://koti.welho.com/jpeltora/littermovement.htm
www.wewanttap.com
www.stickk.com
www.pledgebank.com
www.pgdp.net

47. SWITCH TO GREEN ELECTRICITY

Burning fossil fuels to generate electricity contributes around 30% of our CO_2 emissions. But if you switch to green electricity (which is electricity produced from renewable sources such as solar, wind or wave power), the electricity you consume will have generated no CO_2 at all. So switch right now... and do this on the internet. This is an extremely simple thing that you can do for a better planet.

If switching is going to have any impact, then you need to:

✱ Purchase your electricity from the right supplier – one that is committed to supplying green electricity, and not just doing it as a marketing ploy.

✱ Tell your all friends to switch, and together spread the message as widely as possible.

Compare prices and switch online at *uSwitch*: **www.uswitch.com/gas-electricity/cheaper-green-energy** And at *Gooshing*: **www.gooshing.co.uk/home_energy**

Specialist green energy suppliers include:

✱ *Good Energy*, which supplies all its electricity from renewable sources: **www.goodenergy.co.uk**

✱ *Ecotricity*, which builds its own wind turbine and solar panel generation capacity: **www.ecotricity.co.uk**

✱ *Green Energy*, which obtains its green electricity from wholly British renewable sources, excluding nuclear power; its customers can earn shares in the company: **www.greenenergy.uk.com**

These are the different shades of green energy:
Bright green: Wind turbines, solar-electric, solar heating, hydro-electric and wave power all use natural sources of energy and produce no carbon emissions.

Pale green: Biomass which takes plant material and burns it. Landfill sites and sewage produce methane, which can then be collected and burned. Carbon taken from the atmosphere is returned to it is better than...

Conventional: Burning oil, coal and gas. Burning non-renewable fossil fuel is the major cause of rising carbon levels in the atmosphere. Coal and oil from tar sands are the worst, as these generate a lot of CO_2 for each unit of electricity. Gas is the most efficient.

Nuclear: No carbon is produced in running the power station, but constructing it has a big carbon footprint and the safe disposal of nuclear waste which is a huge and unsolved problem.

CONSUME LESS ELECTRICITY

Switching to green electricity may be the green thing to do, but equally important is to reduce your energy consumption as much you can. Here are some things that you can do:

✱ *Do without air conditioning.* Peel off and sweat it out... or use a more eco-friendly fan system which blows air through water as it drips through dried grass.

✱ *Change all your lightbulbs* to low energy. Lighting accounts for 10-15% of your electricity bill. Using energy-saving light bulbs saves about £10 per bulb per annum and around 75% of your lighting costs. Using LEDs saves even more.

✱ *Turn the lights off* when not needed.

✱ *Go to bed early one night a week*... but make sure that you still have fun!

* *Turn your electronic equipment off* when it is not being used, rather than leaving it on standby. An *IntelliPlug* will help you do this: **www.oneclickpower.co.uk**.

* *Shower* rather than use a bath… and showering with a friend will save another 50%.

* Come up with lots of ideas for *saving energy at your workplace*. Then persuade your boss to put these into practice.

Use Paperless Post: Send a letter to someone telling them that you have switched and asking them to do the same. Do it as an email, but an email that looks and feels like a letter: **www.paperlesspost. com**. And convert your own handwriting into a font in about 15 minutes: **www.writing-fonts.com**

WHAT SHADE OF GREEN ARE YOU?

These are 23 strands of environmentalism based on different social and political viewpoints. What shade of green are you? Have a bit of fun checking out all of these terms on the internet:

Anarcho-primitivism
Blue-green alliance
Bright green environmentalism
Deep ecology
Eco-anarchism
Eco-capitalism
Eco-socialism
Ecocentrism
Ecofascism
Ecofeminism
Environmentalism
Ethicism

Free market environmentalism
Fundi politics
Green anarchism
Green liberalism
Green syndicalism
Hardlne syncretism
Natural capitalism
Radical environmentalism
Red-green alliance
Social ecology
Technogaianism

FINDING OUT WATTSON

If you measure your energy use, you will find it easier to reduce it. A smart meter will measure your total electricity use minute by minute which will encourage you to find ways of consuming less.

One smart meter is the *Wattson* which also records your energy usage over a period of months. You can use *Wattson* to find out how much money each appliance costs to run, and how much it costs when left on standby. You might find, for example, that your microwave costs you £25 a year just to tell the time and waiting for you to ask it to do something.

Wattson is stylishly designed and costs just £100.
Order it at: **www.diykyoto.com**

Click2Change URLs
www.uswitch.com/gas-electricity/cheaper-green-energy
www.gooshing.co.uk/home_energy
www.goodenergy.co.uk
www.ecotricity.co.uk
www.greenenergy.uk.com
www.oneclickpower.co.uk
www.paperlesspost.com
www.writing-fonts.com
www.diykyoto.com

48. CHANGE THE WORLD WITH YOUR CREDIT CARD

There are *charge cards*, where you charge your purchases to your card, but have to pay off any outstanding balance at the end of each month; *debit cards*, where the purchase amount is immediately debited to your bank account; and *credit cards*, where you can maintain an outstanding unpaid balance. The credit card issuer makes money by charging a percentage on transactions and from interest charged on outstanding balances.

Your credit card provides you with an opportunity to do good at no cost. There are thousands credit cards on offer. Some are issued by financial institutions in partnership with a non-profit, the partner getting an up-front fee for every customer joining plus a small percentage of the amount spent on the card. These are called *"Affinity Cards"*.

Before you decide to use an *Affinity Card*, think about these five things:

*   Are you prepared to *forgo the personal benefits*, such as *Air Miles* or *Nectar Points*, that you could get with other cards?

*   Does the card offer *a reasonably good deal on interest charges*?

*   Do you *believe enough in the cause* to want to support it through an affinity card?

*   Does the card *give enough to the cause*? Some give more than others.

*   If you see yourself as an "ethical consumer", wouldn't you want to use *a more ethical card company*?

If you are still keen on having and using an *Affinity Card*, find a charity you like, sign up to its card. Then use it for all your purchases.

Another idea which enables you to give even more is to find the best credit card deal on offer, and then donate all your signing up and cashback benefits to your chosen charity. If you are a U K taxpayer, these donations would also be eligible for *GiftAid*, adding a further 25%.

Find out about the best deals at: **www.moneysavingexpert.com**

AN ETHICAL BANK AND AN AFFINITY CARD

The *Co-operative Bank* has affinity cards supporting *Action Aid, Amnesty, Greenpeace, WaterAid, Save the Children* and other charities. They contribute:

*   £15 for opening the account.

*   Plus £2.50 if you use your account within six months.

*   Plus 25p for every £100 spent.

www.co-operativebank.co.uk

GO RED, GIVE EVEN MORE

The *American Express Red Card* donates 1% of your spend to the *Global Fund* to help fight AIDS, tuberculosis and malaria in Africa, plus another £5 if you use the card in the first month. There is no annual fee.

The RED card is one of several products devised by *(PRODUCT) RED*, created by Bono, lead singer of U2, and Bobby Shriver, Chairman of *DATA* (the *Debt AIDS Trade in Africa* organisation that Bono helped set up) to raise awareness and money for the *Global Fund* by creating joint promotions with leading brands.

You can buy these other RED products:

* A *Motorola* RED mobile phone (£10 donated plus 5% of your bill for calls and texts).

* A RED *iPod Nano* ($10 donated) and then a RED iTunes download card (10% donated).

* A *GAP* INSPI(RED) t-shirt and *Converse* mudcloth leisure shoes.

* *Armani* wrap-around sunglasses (as worn by Bono) tees, vests, underwear, blousons, belts and bags (around 40% donated).

* A set of classic books from *Penguin* (50% of profits donated).

* A *Bugaboo* baby stroller (1% of revenues from all *Bugaboo* products donated to the *Global Fund*). Get your baby firmly grounded in philanthropy!

(PRODUCT) RED: **www.joinred.com/red**
The Global Fund: **www.theglobalfund.org**

Who is Bono? Paul Hewson was born in Dublin on 10th May 1960. He was originally nicknamed "Bono Vox" (good voice) by a friend supposedly after a hearing aid advertisement they passed by regularly and because he sang so loudly that he seemed to be singing for the deaf. He later shortened this to Bono, which he is now known by. He joined U2 in 1976 in response to an advertisement asking for people to form a band, later becoming lead singer. Bono and his fellow Irishman Bob Geldof have played a leading role in campaigning for third world debt relief and a better deal for Africa.

BE A VIRGIN GIVER

The *Virgin Charity Card* pays 0.8% to charity (you can pick from a list), and you can increase this to 1% if you are a UK taxpayer with *GiftAid*. This ends up being equivalent to *American Express*'s 1%, but gives you a choice of charity.

You can support any charity registered with *Virgin Money Giving* (1,500 and growing). You can also get the charity you want to support to register. **http://uk.virginmoney.com**

www.moneysavingexpert.com
www.co-operativebank.co.uk
www.joinred.com/red
www.theglobalfund.org
http://uk.virginmoney.com

49. SHOP ETHICALLY ONLINE

Internet retailing is growing fast. In 2010, 6% of all spending on goods and services in the UK was done online, and there were 25 million online shoppers. You can shop online, and use your consumer pound together with a click of your mouse to make a difference.

But before spending anything, use these criteria for choosing what to purchase if you want to become a "good consumer":

* See what you can *reuse or swap* before deciding to buy something.

* Buy only those things that you *actually need*.

* Buy *local*, and wherever possible *direct* from producers.

* Buy *organic* and *fairly-traded* products where these are available.

* Buy *poison-free* products, important with cotton which you wear next to your skin.

* Buy products which are *cruelty free* – which don't harm animals or involve child labour.

* Buy things which have been *produced sustainably* (wood and paper made from sustainable forests, fish from sustainable fisheries, anything recycled).

* Buy products that have a *longer life* and which can be *disposed of safely* when you have finished with them.

* Buy *more energy efficient* products which have a lower carbon footprint.

* Buy products *made by poor communities* through social enterprises and cooperatives.

You must also like what you buy and the price should be right.

BUY FAIRTRADE

What small producers in poor countries need most is a fair price for their products… plus acceptable working conditions… plus some assurance that there will be a market for what they produce. This is the basis of the *Fairtrade* movement, which mobilises consumers to purchase products which give the producer a fairer deal and encourages retailers and workplaces to stock *Fairtrade* products.

Fairtrade started with tea and coffee sold through charity shops and catalogues. The range now includes coffee, drinking chocolate, chocolate bars, orange juice, tea, honey, sugar and bananas... and even footballs, cotton products and roses. Many supermarkets and retail chains now offer fairly traded merchandise – for example, *Marks & Spencer* and *Starbucks* now only sell fairly traded coffee.

Buy *Fairtrade* if you can to ensure a better deal for producers. Explore the following websites:
Fairtrade Labelling Organisation, the international *Fairtrade* body: **www.fairtrade.net**
Rainforest Alliance, focusing on sustainability and forest produce: **www.rainforest-alliance.org**
Fairtrade towns, schools, universities, workplaces, and how to become one: **www.fairtrade.org.uk**
World Fair Trade Day (second Sunday in May): **www.wftday.org**

BUY ETHICALLY, GO GOOSHING

To find out whether what you are intending to buy is produced by a socially responsible company, you can then use following resources:

Ethical Consumer. Their *Ethiscore Service* provides information for the ethical or green shopper (cost £15 per annum). You get unlimited online access to daily updated versions of all of Buyer's Guides and Reports. *Ethical Consumer* also maintains a list of consumer boycotts with the reasons behind them. **www.ethicalconsumer.org**

The Ethical Company Organisation. This provides clear and comparative ethical shopping information on thousands of companies and brands for ethical shoppers and other socially responsible purchasers. It publishes *"The Good Shopping Guide"* and operates the *Gooshing* internet sales website: **www.ethical-company-organisation.org**
www.gooshing.co.uk

You can also go shopping at:
The Ethical Superstore: **www.ethicalsuperstore.com**
Get Ethical, set up by *The Big Issue* and *Red Pepper* magazines: **www.getethical.com**
Etsy, a website for makers to sell direct to customers: **www.etsy.com**
Traidcraft, a catalogue of fairly traded products: **www.traidcraftshop.co.uk**
E-shop Africa, artisanal products from West Africa: **www.eshopafrica.com**

We live in a world of international brands. You can find out what's **Behind the Label**, which is a US union-sponsored campaign **www.behindthelabel.org**

HELP STAMP OUT SWEATSHOPS

In 160 countries around the world, over 23.6 million people, many of them young women and teenagers, work in garment sweatshops producing cheap clothing for Western consumers. About 80% work under conditions that systematically violate local as well as international laws. Despite promises by the retailers to try to clean up the system, the situation seems to be getting worse, not better, as poor countries compete for low-wage jobs.

The *No Sweat* campaign exposes this exploitation and tries to stamp out sweatshops. Join the campaign. Buy *No Sweat* t-shirts and help get the message across: **www.nosweat.org.uk**

GoodWeave seeks to end child labour in the carpet industry: **www.goodweave.org**

Find out about other things you can do at **www.coopamerica.org/programs/sweatshops/whatyoucando**

Click2Change URLs
www.fairtrade.net
www.rainforest-alliance.org
www.fairtrade.org.uk
www.wftday.org
www.ethicalconsumer.org
www.ethical-company-organisation.org
www.gooshing.co.uk
www.ethicalsuperstore.com
www.getethical.com
www.etsy.com
www.traidcraftshop.co.uk
www.eshopafrica.com
www.behindthelabel.org
www.nosweat.org.uk
www.goodweave.org
www.coopamerica.org/programs/sweatshops/whatyoucando
www.greenknickers.org
www.pantstopoverty.com

AND JUST FOR A BIT OF FUN...

Buy yourself some *Green Knickers* (or boxers) and buy a second pair for your partner or loved one. These are ethical knickers with a twist. Or say *"Pants to Poverty"* by buying a pair of *Pants to Poverty* underpants for men and women. Both these are organic and fairly traded. **www.greenknickers.org** and **www.pantstopoverty.com**

50. REDUCE YOUR FOOD MILES

How much of the food you ate today was grown locally? And how much travelled hundreds or even thousands of miles to reach your table? Imported food has to travel by air, ship and road to get to you. Even food grown in your own country has to travel from farm to distribution centre and then to the supermarket or shop where you purchase it. The carbon footprint of all this travel is a major contributor to global warming, but also adds to congestion and pollution.

In the UK, 95% of fruit and 50% of vegetables are imported. The amount of food being flown in by air is rising each year. Food is also travelling further within the UK largely because supermarkets have centralised their distribution systems. Agriculture and food now account for nearly 30% of goods transported on our roads.

With manufactured food, the ingredients will have travelled still further – from factory to factory before they end up on the supermarket shelf. Researchers in Britain and Germany found that to produce a small glass jar of strawberry yogurt on sale in Stuttgart, strawberries were transported from Poland to West Germany and then processed into jam and sent to southern Germany. Yogurt cultures came from North Germany, corn and wheat flour from the Netherlands, sugar beet from East Germany, and the labels and aluminium covers for the jars were made over 300km away. Only the glass jar and the milk were produced locally. To get one lorry-load of yogurt pots to the south German distribution centre involved the equivalent of one lorry travelling a distance of over 1,000 kilometres consuming 400 litres of diesel. Take any product, and you will find much the same story.

Make a difference by making these choices:

1. Shop locally. Next best, buy online.

2. Buy fresh ingredients to cook at home. Join an organic box scheme, such as *Riverford Organics* or *Abel & Cole*: **www.riverford.co.uk** and **www.abelandcole.co.uk**. Find a farmers market near you: **www.localfoods.org.uk/local-food-directory**

3. Cut down on food waste and compost what's left over. The average household throws away more than 3kgs of food per week.

FOOD MILE MADNESS

A *Guardian* reporter bought a basket of 20 fresh food items and calculated the foodmiles involved: apples from America; pears from Argentina; fish from the Indian ocean; lettuce from Spain; tomatoes from Saudi Arabia; broccoli from Spain; baby carrots from South Africa; salad potatoes from Israel; sugar snap peas from Guatemala; asparagus from Peru, garden peas from South Africa; red wine from Chile; Brussels sprouts from Australia; prawns from Indonesia; chicken from Thailand; red peppers from Holland; grapes from Chile; strawberries from Spain and beef from Britain. The items in the basket had travelled a total of 100,943 miles.

Sustain advocates food and agriculture practice that enhances the health and welfare of people and animals. Take a look at their *FoodFacts*: **www.sustainweb.org**. Check out *Grassroots Action on Food and Farming*: **www.gaff.org.uk**

Here are four things you can do, three of them from your computer:

1. **Become more aware.** With four friends, each go shopping on-line at your favourite supermarket, each with £20 to spend (not including delivery) purchasing at least 10 items. Your challenge is to spend your money on produce that has travelled the furthest to get to you. Multiply the weight of each pack (in kilograms) by distance travelled (in miles). See who can clock up the most kilogram-miles. Winner takes all. You'll end up with a better understanding of food mile madness.

2. **Change how you eat.** Restrict your food miles. Always ask where produce has come from. Make a rule never to buy anything that has travelled further than 100 miles. You won't starve. In 2005 Alisa Smith and James MacKinnon ate only local food for one year, and wrote about their experiences in "*The Hundred Mile Diet*". In 2008, they challenged the people of Mission, British Columbia to do take the *Mission 100 Challenge*. Take the pledge to eat local at: **http://100mile.foodtv.ca**

3. **Take action.** Design and print some labels on your computer with these messages: "*Environmental madness*". "*Do not buy this product*". "*Too many food miles*". Take them with you when you next go to the supermarket…

4. **Put pressure on your local supermarket** to purchase locally. Ask them to clearly mark air-freighted produce and to purchase more foods grown within a 30-mile radius and mark these as of local origin. Get contact details from their website, or write to the Chairman's office.

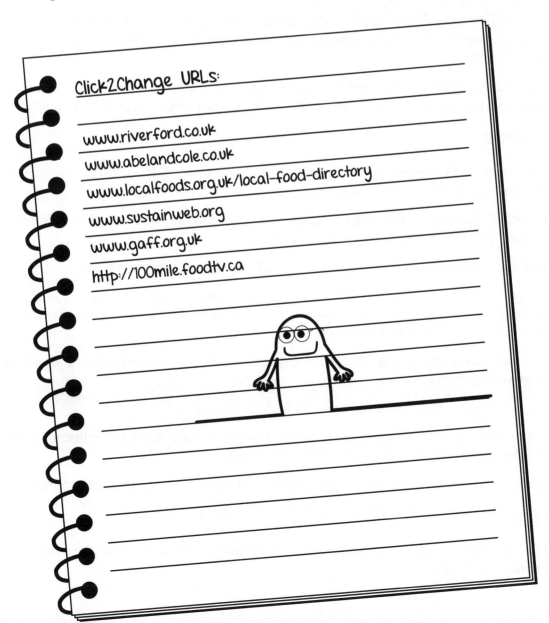

Click2Change URLs:

www.riverford.co.uk
www.abelandcole.co.uk
www.localfoods.org.uk/local-food-directory
www.sustainweb.org
www.gaff.org.uk
http://100mile.foodtv.ca

51. BECOME A SOCIAL BANKER

Do you really want to deposit your money with a high street bank – those same banks which were at the epicentre of the 2008 financial meltdown and which had to be bailed out with "our money"? The interest you get on your savings will be pretty well zero, and your money is more likely to be used to support hedge funds and transnational takeovers than to lend to small businesses and kickstart the economy. Check out some of these alternatives.

And find out more about the 2008 financial crisis: **http://en.wikipedia.org/wiki/Financial_crisis**

USE AN ETHICAL BANK

Instead of using a regular commercial bank, such as *Citibank* (the world's largest) or *HSBC* (which calls itself "the world's local bank"), use a bank which is a mutual or cooperative (which means that it doesn't pay dividends to shareholders), or a bank which has a commitment to using their money in a socially responsible way. Check out the following.

In the UK, the *Co-operative Bank* is part of the *Co-operative Movement*, together with its *"Smile"* online banking operation. Both make a commitment to use your money ethically. **www.co-operativebank. co.uk** and **www.smile.co.uk**

Other UK ethical banks include *Triodos Bank* **www.triodos.co.uk**, and the *Ecology Building Society* **www. ecology.co.uk**. Both use your money to finance projects which are of social and environmental benefit.

PEER-TO-PEER LENDING

Social lending directly links lenders with borrowers (that's peer to peer). If you do this, you can choose who to lend to, and you will get better rates than you can get commercially.

Zopa was the world's first social lending marketplace. It launched in the UK in 2005. This is how it works:

1. To get started, you sign up by registering your details.
2. Loan applicants are credit scored. They are A*, A, B, C-rated or young (age 20-25).
3. Lenders choose the level of risk and the interest rate, the period of the loan (3 or 5 years), and the amount they wish to lend (from £10 upwards). – *"I'd like to lend this much to A-rated borrowers for this long which will get me this rate."*
4. To reduce risk, only small amounts are lent to any one borrower. A lender lending £500 or more has the money spread across 50 borrowers.
5. Borrowers enter into legally binding contracts with their lenders.
6. Borrowers repay monthly by direct debit. If any repayments are missed, a collections agency is used – the same recovery process used by high street banks.
7. *Zopa* charges borrowers a 0.5% transaction fee and lenders a 0.5% annual service charge.
8. The transaction is completed online… not a bank manager in sight!

Lend through *Zopa*. Open an account today. Put your savings to work to help people succeed in their business and improve their lives…

... and earn a good rate of interest at the same time (average lending rates were 7.5% after fees but before allowing for bad debt). Why not try it out with £50? **http://uk.zopa.com**

Social banking is spreading around the world. Check out the following (also in the UK):

Funding Circle lends to small businesses. You earn a 8.3% return plus a 0.5% cashback on your investment through funding circle. Your lending is spread across lots of businesses to reduce risk. **www.fundingcircle.com**

RateSetter, where borrowers advertise what rates they are prepared to pay. You can accept the rates on offer or set the rate at which you wish to lend and wait for a borrower prepared to pay this. They also have a *"Rolling Monthly Fund"* to spread the risk: **www.ratesetter.com**

Lending In US dollars:
Prosper: **www.prosper.com** and *Lending Club:* **www.lendingclub.com**
Other US based services are *Vittana*, *United Prosperity*, *Zidisha* (all microfinance) and *People Capital* (student loans).

Lending In Canadian dollars:
CommunityLend: **www.communitylend.com**

Lending In Euros:
Smava, Germany: **www.smava.de**. *Boober*, Italy: **www.boober.it**. *Pret d'union*, France: **www.pret-dunion.fr**

START YOUR OWN BANK

MyBnk allows young people to run their own bank, to save with and to borrow from, to learn about money and enterprise, and to do it for real. A *MyBnk* bank is controlled by a committee of young people, who promote the bank in their school, encourage borrowing and decide who to lend to and what for. Borrowers do not pay interest, but they pay back with ideas, time and by helping someone else. There is *"MyBnk in a Box"*, which is a toolkit to help you set up your *MyBnk*. Start your own *MyBnk*. View the *"Video Hotseats"*, where people talk about how enterprise changed their lives.

Learn to be an entrepreneur with *Enterprise-in-a-Box*: **www.mybnk.org** and **www.enterpriseinabox.org**

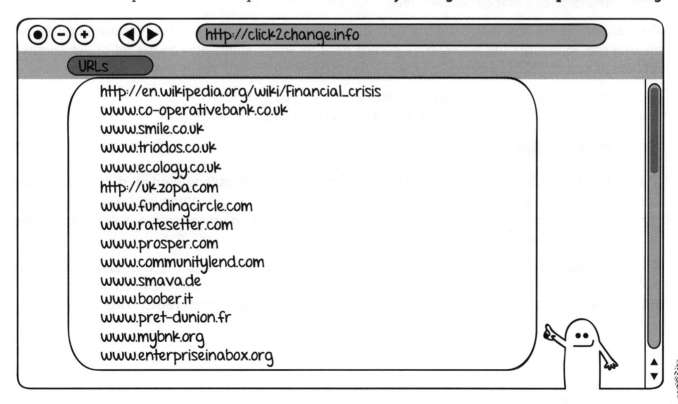

http://click2change.info

URLs

http://en.wikipedia.org/wiki/Financial_crisis
www.co-operativebank.co.uk
www.smile.co.uk
www.triodos.co.uk
www.ecology.co.uk
http://uk.zopa.com
www.fundingcircle.com
www.ratesetter.com
www.prosper.com
www.communitylend.com
www.smava.de
www.boober.it
www.pret-dunion.fr
www.mybnk.org
www.enterpriseinabox.org

52. GIVE A GOOD GIFT

There are all sorts of occasions when you need to give someone a present… birthdays, Christmas, Mother's or Father's Day, Valentine's Day, weddings, a special night out with your sweetheart, an in-memoriam gift for someone who has died, because you've just been promoted, going-home presents at children's parties, or just because you feel like giving somebody something.

How often do you find that you can't think what to give? How often have you given (or been given) something that they or you don't need and don't like… which is then quietly hidden away and forgotten, or taken to a charity shop, or passed on to somebody else as a present (which they won't like either!), or sold on eBay?

So here's a really great alternative. *BUY A GOOD GIFT*.

This is how it works. Choose a gift from a catalogue. Your gift is in fact just a charitable donation, but a donation which enables something very specific to happen which will do real good in the world. Here is a selection of ideas from the *Good Gifts Catalogue*:

Bamboo Bikes: Stronger than traditional steel, bikes, and cheaper too, buy a bamboo bike for a Ghana midwife (£45) which will enable her to get around more quickly… express delivery!

Save the Rainforest: Buy half an acre (£25) – that's all it costs!

Goats for Peace: Provide a revolving goat to support a family – they keep the milk, but sell the kids (£20).

Gift of Sight: Pay for a simple operation to restore the sight of someone suffering from cataracts, trachoma or other blinding conditions (£27).

Turning Homeless People Green: Buy them allotment equipment (£45) so they can grow their own fruit and veg – pot-handling rather than pan-handling!

Donkey-Drawn Libraries in war-torn Africa: (£100) or a ***Book Grant*** (£35). Books give people ideas… and ideas can change people's lives.

The recipient gets a card with details of how their gift is helping. They will take pleasure in helping making someone else's life better. They do not need to worry about how to get rid of yet another unwanted and unneeded present. They will love your gift, which will really make a difference.

Good Gifts Catalogue (UK): **www.goodgifts.org**
Changing the Present (USA): **www.changingthepresent.org**

ALTERNATIVE GIFTS MARKETS

In 1980 Harriet Prichard held an "alternative gifts" market at the Pasadena Presbyterian Church, California where things and animals benefiting needy people in the developing world were sold. It was organised rather like a Christmas crafts fair. Cards inscribed by hand for each gift purchased were sent to the recipient telling them of the gift given in their honour.

The idea spread. Today, some 350 markets are organised each year across the USA and in England, Holland, Japan and Korea. *Alternative Gifts International* can help you organise your own alternative gifts market. There is also a catalogue of gifts to buy online. **www.alternativegifts.org**

WHAT'S THE STUPIDEST GIFT YOU'VE EVER RECEIVED?

So much money is spent on ridiculous gifts. Changing the Present's *Stupid Gift Hall of Shame* features some real horrors. Here are some:

* A telephone handset that plugs into a mobile, so you feel that you are speaking on a landline.

* A baby's dummy in the shape of a prickly cactus.

* A note-holder that keeps your notes literally in front of your eyes.

* A mask for a dog, so it can pretend to be a cat.

What's the stupidest gift you have ever received? Is it stupider than any of these? Submit your stupid gift to the *Hall of Shame*. You could win a prize – if it's stupid enough! **www.changingthepresent.org**

WOULD YOU RATHER?

Life is all about options. We can't do or have everything we want. So we make choices. For example, instead of taking a weekend break in the South of France and flying there with a budget airline, spend the weekend having a holiday at home and giving yourself lots of treats (visit that art exhibition you've been wanting to go to, spend an afternoon being pampered in a health spa…), and then donate what you have saved to fighting climate change. You will feel refreshed in all senses.

Spend less and make a good gift with what you haven't spent. *Alternative Gifts International* suggests these choices:

* *For the cost of a ten-piece chicken dinner,* provide a smoke-free stove for a needy Haitian family.

* *For the cost of a pedicure,* send 50 kilos of milled rice to hungry Filipino villagers.

* *For the cost of a household microwave oven,* donate a refrigeration unit to a Peruvian farmer for their cheese-making business.

New Message

File   Edit   View   Insert   Format   Tools   Message   Help

Send

From: click2change@gmail.com

To:

Cc:

Subject: URLs

www.goodgifts.org
www.changingthepresent.org
www.alternativegifts.org

DOOMSDAY IS COMING

We've been encouraging you to do something to make a better world... but will the world as we know it survive? Or will our planet come to an untimely end caused by one of the many threats facing it?

"The Doomsday Book: Scenarios for the End of the World" analyses the threats facing the planet, which could obliterate life as we know it. These include:

✳ Nanotechnology and artificial intelligence getting out of control and biting back at us.

✳ A global pandemic, maybe caused by a superbug, that kills off all humankind.

✳ A third and final world war, caused by nations competing to rule the world, or through global terror sparked off by extremism and fundamentalism.

✳ The poisoning of the planet with pesticides and pollutants and all the chemicals we now use.

✳ The planet running out of water, and the land losing its fertility.

✳ The hydroxyl time bomb when the atmosphere's self-regulating processes for cleaning the air stop working.

✳ Climate change fuelled by greenhouse gas emissions causing rising sea levels through polar icecaps and glaciers melting.

✳ Marine life disappearing through over-exploitation of the oceans, and the acidification of sea water as carbon dioxide levels rise.

✳ A new ice age caused by the shutting down of the gulf stream, another possible outcome of global warming.

✳ Comet and asteroid impacts, or some other cosmological catastrophe.

✳ A mega-tsunami obliterating all the land in its path or a super volcano spewing larva into the atmosphere which cuts off the sunlight needed to sustain life.

What is the seriousness of these threats? What is the likelihood anything happening? Should we be worried?

1. Read *The Doomsday Book* by Joel Levy. Make up your own mind as to whether the planet has a future worth bothering about. Decide whether you should be doing something to make life better or simply enjoying life on earth whilst it lasts.

2. Find out about the risks to human beings, civilisation and the planet at: **http://en.wikipedia.org/wiki/End_of_civilization**

3. Browse the *Doomsday Guide*, the ultimate guide to the ultimate end: **www.doomsdayguide.org/doomsday_scenarios.htm**

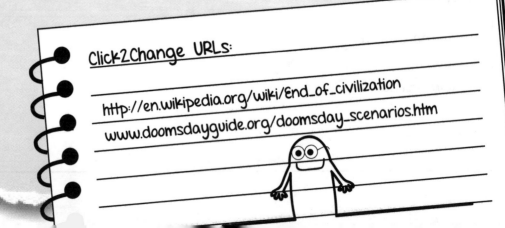

Click2Change URLs:

http://en.wikipedia.org/wiki/End_of_civilization

www.doomsdayguide.org/doomsday_scenarios.htm

RESIGN YOUR JOB

Are you doing what you really want to be doing? Or is there something more interesting and more useful that you would like to do with your life? Do you feel trapped and unable to make a decision to break out?

Think about this. It may be that you could direct yourself and your energy and your ideas more fruitfully on changing the world for the better. If this is the case, then break free. Resign your job. Don't delay – do it today!

And whilst you are changing the course of your life, downshift your lifestyle. Here are seven ways for slowing down and greening up suggested by *International Downshifting Week*: **www.downshiftingweek.com**

1. **Money:** *Cut up your Credit card*

The more money you spend, the longer you need to work to pay for it.
Remember: The very best things in life are free.

2. **Time:** *Reclaim an hour of time this week*

What's the point money, it you haven't the time to spend it?
Remember: The most important gift of all is time.

3. **Waste:** *Start composting or recycling*

Get a handle on refuse and energy use. Watch your waste.
Remember: Landfill is one stroke away from land full.

4. **Giving:** *Donate time or things to a worthy cause*

Make this your year to volunteer.
Remember: Kindness is infectious. Give someone else the bug.

5. **Food:** *Cook a simple meal using fresh local ingredients*

Peel it, chop it, stir it, stuff it, love it!
Remember: Ditch the fear and indulge in the fun and fantasy of simple home cooking.

6. **Community:** *Purchase local produce from a local shop*

It's time to explore our super markets!
Remember: A high street without decent, local shops, is a street that's lost it's high.

7. **Enjoy:** *Start doing something that you really want to do*

There is a life outside of the commute which will unleash your concealed talents.
Remember: How will you ever know what lies within, unless you make the time to scratch the surface?

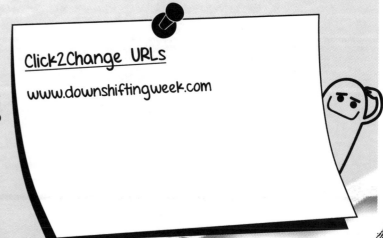

Click2Change URLs

www.downshiftingweek.com

BE A HYPOCRITE

There are lots of things that we all do which we know we shouldn't be doing. And despite being told again and again that these are wrong, we continue doing them.

There's always going to be some part of us that says *"Hey, let's party and have a good time!"*. Life is there to be enjoyed, and we can't be expected to turn the thermostat down and shiver in the cold or just wear hand-me-downs all the time. But we do need to create a better balance between how we live our lives and our social and environmental responsibilities to the wider world.

Here is a recipe for how we might all become a little less hypocritical:

1. ***Be a hypocrite.*** Start by recognising that we all do and will continue to do things that we know we shouldn't be doing. We continue spreading the message of global warming, yet still take flights to Ibiza. We continue consuming as if the world had unlimited resources, forgetting the difference between "needs" and "wants".

2. ***Own up to your hypocrisies.*** Next make a list of all your smaller and bigger acts of hypocrisy which contribute towards making the world a bit worse instead of a bit better, things you are doing that you know in your heart of hearts that you really shouldn't be doing.

3. ***Commit yourself to one less hypocrisy.*** Pledge to *stop doing* or to *do much less of* one of the things on your list… this will be your first small step towards becoming less of a hypocrite.

4. ***Repeat the process.*** Having done taken this first step, look at your list and select one more thing to do… and do it. Continue this process until you have gone through the whole of your list.

Why not a *National Hypocrisy Day*? One day each year when everyone from Prime Minster to pensioner is asked to "come out" with their hypocrisies, and pledge to stop doing just one… let's find a way of taking this idea forward.

LET'S GO TO MARS

Mars is a fascinating place. It has volcanoes bigger than Mount Everest and canyons bigger than the Grand Canyon. It may once have been – and indeed may still be – a life-bearing planet. It's a world ripe for exploration and discovery.

If we have trashed the Earth so that it becomes uninhabitable, perhaps Mars will provide a solution – at least for those who can get there. This will require technological innovation on a huge scale to travel there and to set up home on the planet.

This is an extract from the declaration by the 1998 Founding Convention of the Mars Society:

The time has come for humanity to journey to Mars. Though Mars is distant, we are far better prepared today to send humans to Mars than we were to travel to the Moon at the commencement of the space age. We're ready.

* ***We must go for the knowledge of Mars.*** *Robotic probes have revealed that Mars was once a warm and wet planet, suitable for hosting life's origin. But did it?*

* ***We must go for the knowledge of Earth.*** *Mars, the planet most like Earth, will teach us about our home world. This knowledge could be key to our survival.*

* ***We must go for the challenge.*** *Cooperative international exploration of Mars could serve as an example of how the same joint-action could be made to work on Earth.*

* ***We must go for the opportunity.*** *Settling the Martian New World is an opportunity for a noble experiment in which humanity has a chance to begin the world anew.*

* ***We must go for our humanity.*** *We have the ability to continue the work of creation by bringing life to Mars, and Mars to life.*

* ***We must go for the future.*** *Mars is a New World, filled with history waiting to be made.*

Mars Society, USA: **www.marssociety.org**
NASA's *Be A Martian* website: **http://beamartian.jpl.nasa.gov**

Alternatively, there's a possibility that you could be abducted by an alien. Check out: **http://en.wikipedia.org/wiki/Alien_abduction** and **www.abduct.com**

To prepare for your life on Mars, read: *"Packing for Mars: The Curious Science of Life in the Void"*: **www.maryroach.net/packing-for-mars.html**

Click2Change URLs

www.marssociety.org
http://beamartian.jpl.nasa.gov
http://en.wikipedia.org/wiki/Alien_abduction
www.abduct.com
www.maryroach.net/packing-for-mars.html

MAKE A PLEDGE

You've read the book. You now know that you can do lots of little things to change the world – from your desktop or *iPhone*, and without even getting off your backside. Now's the time to decide to address some of the issues and problems you really care about. Make a pledge to make a difference.

PLEDGE TO MAKE A DIFFERENCE

I pledge to do what I can to change the world for the better.

These are the issues that I really care about:

1.
2.
3.
4.

These are the five things that I pledge to do to address these issues:

1.
2.
3.
4.
5.

Signed: Date:

Now turn your pledges into action. We wish you every success with your attempts to change the world.

Multiply the impact of what you are doing. Put your pledge on *PledgeBank* and invite other people to pledge to do the same things: **www.pledgebank.org**

Get help in sticking to your pledges. Go to **www.stickk.com** to create a support network and give yourself rewards and punishments for success or failure.

Sign up for a daily email or tweet. Tell us about your ideas and your achievements.
Our best wishes for your world-changing efforts. You can contact us at **www.click2change.net**